Immigration

Other Books in the Current Controversies Series

Assisted Suicide

Developing Nations

E-books

Family Violence

Gays in the Military

Global Warming

Human Trafficking

The Iranian Green Movement

Jobs in America

Medical Ethics

Modern-Day Piracy

Oil Spills

Pakistan

Politics and Religion

Pollution

Rap and Hip-Hop

Vaccines

Violence in the Media

Women in Politics

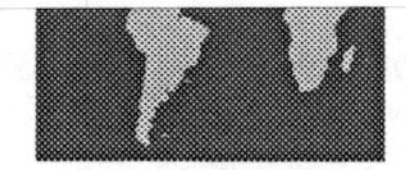

Immigration

Debra A. Miller, Book Editor

GREENHAVEN PRESS
A part of Gale, Cengage Learning

Farmington Hills, Mich • San Francisco • New York • Waterville, Maine
Meriden, Conn • Mason, Ohio • Chicago

Elizabeth Des Chenes, *Director, Content Strategy*
Cynthia Sanner, *Publisher*
Douglas Dentino, *Manager, New Product*

WCN: 01-100-101

For more information, contact:
Greenhaven Press
27500 Drake Rd.
Farmington Hills, MI 48331-3535
Or you can visit our Internet site at gale.cengage.com

Articles in Greenhaven Press anthologies are often edited for length to meet page requirements. In addition, original titles of these works are changed to clearly present the main thesis and to explicitly indicate the author's opinion. Every effort is made to ensure that Greenhaven Press accurately reflects the original intent of the authors. Every effort has been made to trace the owners of copyrighted material.

LIBRARY OF CONGRESS CATALOGING-IN-PUBLICATION DATA

Immigration / Debra A. Miller, book editor.
pages cm. -- (Current controversies)
Summary: "Current Controversies: Immigration This series covers today's most current national and international issues and the most important opinions of the past and present. The purpose of the series is to introduce readers to all sides of contemporary controversies"-- Provided by publisher.
Includes bibliographical references and index.
ISBN 978-0-7377-6874-9 (hardback) -- ISBN 978-0-7377-6875-6 (paperback)
1. United States--Emigration and immigration--Government policy. 2. United States--Emigration and immigration--Social aspects. 3. United States--Emigration and immigration--Political aspects. I. Miller, Debra A., editor of compilation.
JV6450.I559 2014
325.73--dc23

2013041534

Printed in the United States of America
1 2 3 4 5 6 7 18 17 16 15 14

Contents

Foreword

By definition, controversies are "discussions of questions in which opposing opinions clash" (*Webster's Twentieth Century Dictionary Unabridged*). Few would deny that controversies are a pervasive part of the human condition and exist on virtually every level of human enterprise. Controversies transpire between individuals and among groups, within nations and between nations. Controversies supply the grist necessary for progress by providing challenges and challengers to the status quo. They also create atmospheres where strife and warfare can flourish. A world without controversies would be a peaceful world; but it also would be, by and large, static and prosaic.

The Series' Purpose

The purpose of the Current Controversies series is to explore many of the social, political, and economic controversies dominating the national and international scenes today. Titles selected for inclusion in the series are highly focused and specific. For example, from the larger category of criminal justice, Current Controversies deals with specific topics such as police brutality, gun control, white collar crime, and others. The debates in Current Controversies also are presented in a useful, timeless fashion. Articles and book excerpts included in each title are selected if they contribute valuable, long-range ideas to the overall debate. And wherever possible, current information is enhanced with historical documents and other relevant materials. Thus, while individual titles are current in focus, every effort is made to ensure that they will not become quickly outdated. Books in the Current Controversies series will remain important resources for librarians, teachers, and students for many years.

In addition to keeping the titles focused and specific, great care is taken in the editorial format of each book in the series. Book introductions and chapter prefaces are offered to provide background material for readers. Chapters are organized around several key questions that are answered with diverse opinions representing all points on the political spectrum. Materials in each chapter include opinions in which authors clearly disagree as well as alternative opinions in which authors may agree on a broader issue but disagree on the possible solutions. In this way, the content of each volume in Current Controversies mirrors the mosaic of opinions encountered in society. Readers will quickly realize that there are many viable answers to these complex issues. By questioning each author's conclusions, students and casual readers can begin to develop the critical thinking skills so important to evaluating opinionated material.

Current Controversies is also ideal for controlled research. Each anthology in the series is composed of primary sources taken from a wide gamut of informational categories including periodicals, newspapers, books, US and foreign government documents, and the publications of private and public organizations. Readers will find factual support for reports, debates, and research papers covering all areas of important issues. In addition, an annotated table of contents, an index, a book and periodical bibliography, and a list of organizations to contact are included in each book to expedite further research.

Perhaps more than ever before in history, people are confronted with diverse and contradictory information. During the Persian Gulf War, for example, the public was not only treated to minute-to-minute coverage of the war, it was also inundated with critiques of the coverage and countless analyses of the factors motivating US involvement. Being able to sort through the plethora of opinions accompanying today's major issues, and to draw one's own conclusions, can be a complicated and frustrating struggle. It is the editors' hope that Current Controversies will help readers with this struggle.

Introduction

> *"In the latter half of the twentieth century, the nation witnessed a new phenomenon of illegal immigration—immigrants coming mostly from Mexico."*

America has historically been a land of immigrants. From its founding in the colonial era to the 1920s, the United States welcomed a wave of immigrants—first mostly from northwestern European countries such as England, Ireland, France, and Germany and later from Italy, Poland, Russia, and other parts of eastern Europe. Also during this period hundreds of thousands of African slaves were brought to the country against their will. Individual states regulated immigration during the nation's early years. The first significant federal immigration law was the 1882 Chinese Exclusion Act, but in 1921 the US government created a quota system that placed numerical limits on immigration according to nationality; this law strongly favored immigrants from northwestern Europe. The Immigration Act of 1965 ended this discriminatory national-origins quota system and created a system that gave preference to family members of US citizens or legal residents, retaining limits on overall immigration numbers. In the latter half of the twentieth century, the nation witnessed a new phenomenon of illegal immigration—immigrants coming mostly from Mexico. The Immigration Reform and Control Act of 1986 (IRCA) tried to address this issue by granting amnesty to approximately three million unauthorized immigrants already living in the United States at that time, while creating sanctions against employers who knowingly hired illegal immigrants. In recent decades, however, immigrants have continued to enter the United States illegally, prompting policy makers to once again consider immigration reform legislation. Not surprisingly, the scope and characteristics of current immigration to the United States have recently been the subject of much interest.

According to an analysis of US Census Bureau data by the Pew Research Center, a nonpartisan research organization, the total US immigrant population—both legal and unauthorized immigrants—has grown over the last decade to a record 40.4 million in 2011. This means that immigrants now make up about 13 percent of the total US population, lower than the past peak of 15 percent in 1890, which occurred during the earlier period of high immigration from Europe. This modern immigration wave, unlike the first tide of mostly European immigrants, has been dominated by people from Latin America (about 50 percent) and Asia (27 percent).

Census data shows that Mexico is the country of origin for about 29 percent of the immigrants residing in the United States (or about 11.7 million)—clearly the largest US immigrant group. These Mexican immigrants live mostly in the west and southwest parts of the country—in states like California (37 percent), Texas (21 percent), and Arizona (4 percent)—but also in several other states such as Illinois (6 percent) and Georgia (2 percent). Other countries, such as China (5 percent), India (4 percent), the Philippines (4 percent), Vietnam (3 percent), El Salvador (3 percent), Cuba (3 percent), Korea (3 percent), the Dominican Republic (2 percent), and Guatemala (2 percent), make up another 29 percent of the immigrant population.

The majority of new immigrants are young or middle-aged—72 percent are twenty-five to sixty-four years old, 9 percent eighteen to twenty-four years old, and 7 percent age seventeen or younger. Only 13 percent were sixty-five or older. A little more than half of these immigrants are female. About 17.5 million out of 40.4 million are naturalized US citizens, and the rest are legal permanent residents—legal residents here on temporary student or work visas—or unauthorized immigrants. About 47 percent of the total foreign-born population in the United States is Hispanic, and Spanish is the leading second language spoken after English. Out of the 33.6 million immigrants over the age of twenty-five, about a quarter, or 27 percent, have a college degree while a third, or about 32 percent, do not even have a high school diploma.

The main statistic that has been in the news recently, however, is the number of unauthorized or illegal immigrants. According to Jeffrey Passel, a demographer with the Pew Hispanic Center, a project of the nonpartisan Pew Research Center, there are now 11.1 million immigrants living in the United States illegally. This figure is down from a peak of about twelve million in 2007, largely because of decreased immigration from Mexico due to the US recession and stricter border enforcement. In fact, the majority of all unauthorized immigrants come from Mexico—about 58 percent of all unauthorized immigrants (or six million) as of 2010. About half (46 percent) of these unauthorized immigrants have children, some of whom are themselves illegal but many of whom were born in the United States and are therefore US citizens, even though their parents are not legal residents. According to Passel, there are about 4.5 million US citizen children with undocumented parents.

Almost two-thirds of unauthorized immigrants appear to have permanently settled in the United States—they have been here for ten years or more. According to some estimates, up to 40 percent are people who came to the country under a legal visa but then stayed after their visa expired. Many unauthorized immigrants work as low-wage farm workers, helping to pick America's food crops. Others have found niches in the construction industry, dairy operations, or meat-packing plants. Many adult illegal immigrants are poorly educated—about 47 percent have less than a high school education. Many live in poverty and make far less than the $50,000 median annual income for US-born residents.

How to deal with this phenomenon of illegal immigration is a central issue in today's immigration debate, along with other issues such as how the United States should structure its immigration policies to attract more highly skilled and highly educated immigrants. The authors of the viewpoints included in *Current Controversies: Immigration* address some of these topics, including whether immigration is a serious problem, whether the US government adequately enforces immigration laws, whether illegal immigrants should be granted a path to citizenship, and whether immigration reform will improve the US immigration system.

CHAPTER 1

Is Immigration a Serious Problem in the United States?

Chapter Preface

The debate about immigration concerns a critical federal policy matter but it is being fueled by both demographics and politics. Demographers agree that America's white population is slowly aging and shrinking while its Hispanic and Asian American population is younger and growing. This growth in the non-white population is occurring both because new immigrants to the country are overwhelmingly Hispanic or Asian and because the non-white group of American residents is reproducing at a rapid rate. And these demographic changes are being reflected in recent political elections. According to NBC News, whites made up more than 80 percent of all voters in 2000 but by 2004, the white vote had dropped to 77 percent, and in 2008, it declined even more to 74 percent. If this trend continues, NBC predicts that the white vote percentage might sink to 68 percent by 2020. Future elections, therefore, may be decided based on which political party the growing non-white population supports. And immigration reform, many political observers believe, may be one of those issues that will help determine whether non-whites vote mostly for Democrats or Republicans.

The 2012 presidential election, for example, proved to be a bellwether for how demographics might influence politics. Incumbent president Barack Obama, a Democrat, won just 39 percent of the white vote in this election, yet he attracted a huge share of the non-white vote. *The New York Times* reported that approximately 71 percent of Hispanic voters and 73 percent of Asian American voters cast ballots for President Obama, giving him a majority of the popular vote and a win over Republican presidential candidate Mitt Romney. Candidate Romney won only 27 percent of the Hispanic vote, far less even than the 41 percent garnered by Republican president George W. Bush in 2004. A number of commentators have credited President Obama's win to his support for comprehensive immigration reform and his efforts to help undocumented youths avoid deportation, as well as to Mr. Romney's anti-immigrant rhetoric. Candidate Romney, for example, called for self-deportation—a policy of strong immigration enforcement that would encourage unauthorized immigrants to leave the country voluntarily. Many in the Latino community found this to be offensive because it would likely mean insensitive workplace and home raids that would separate families and treat undocumented immigrants inhumanely. And polls confirm that at this point in history, Democratic policies generally seem to appeal to minorities more than Republican ideas. If this trend continues, Democrats may be on track to capture future presidential elections in 2016 and 2020.

Immigration reform legislation appears to have a chance in Congress in the near future largely because leaders in both the Democratic and Republican parties believe such legislation will later translate into Hispanic and Asian votes. Democrats want to maintain their edge with Latinos and Asians while many Republicans feel their party must change its focus in order to woo these minorities. A central part of the reform equation, for example, concerns the question of how to respond to the eleven million undocumented immigrants in the United States, about eight million of whom are Hispanic and 1.3 million of whom are Asian and Pacific Islanders, according to the US Department of Homeland Security. Most Democrats tend to support legalization and a path to citizenship for these immigrants, while Republicans are divided—with many Republican leaders, like Florida senator Marco Rubio, embracing a path to citizenship and others resisting such a policy. While support for immigration reform and a path to citizenship may or may not attract votes, some polls have clearly shown that if either party is seen to be blocking immigration reform, votes could be lost.

The bigger question, however, is what effect today's immigration policies may have on the country in the more distant future. If immigration from Mexico is slowed, or if economic development and declining birthrates in Mexico persist, America's Latino population could stabilize. If the family preference in current immigration law is modified, that also could mean fewer Hispanic entrants. On the other hand, if immigration reform results in more visas for high-skilled workers, that could mean a greater increase in Asian immigrants, who typically tend to be highly educated with valuable skills. Another issue centers on the question of how quickly newly admitted immigrants and their children are able to achieve education and income levels that will lift them into the American middle class. Some observers worry that many of the undocumented immigrants who could be legalized by an immigration reform bill have little education and few skills, and therefore may turn out to be a drain on the US treasury rather than a benefit to the economy.

The authors of the viewpoints in this chapter address the threshold question of whether immigration is a serious problem in the United States, revealing wide differences of opinion on how to respond to both illegal and legal immigration issues.

Illegal Immigration Creates Large Fiscal Costs for US Taxpayers

Robert Rector and Jason Richwine

Robert Rector is a senior research fellow in the department of domestic policy studies at The Heritage Foundation, a conservative think tank. Jason Richwine is a former senior policy analyst for empirical studies at the Foundation.

Unlawful immigration and amnesty for current unlawful immigrants can pose large fiscal costs for U.S. taxpayers. Government provides four types of benefits and services that are relevant to this issue:

- *Direct benefits.* These include Social Security, Medicare, unemployment insurance, and workers' compensation.
- *Means-tested welfare benefits.* There are over 80 of these programs which, at a cost of nearly $900 billion per year, provide cash, food, housing, medical, and other services to roughly 100 million low-income Americans. Major programs include Medicaid, food stamps, the refundable Earned Income Tax Credit, public housing, Supplemental Security Income, and Temporary Assistance for Needy Families.
- *Public education.* At a cost of $12,300 per pupil per year, these services are largely free or heavily subsidized for low-income parents.
- *Population-based services.* Police, fire, highways, parks, and similar services, as the National Academy of Sci-

Robert Rector and Jason Richwine, "The Fiscal Cost of Unlawful Immigrants and Amnesty to the U.S. Taxpayer," *The Heritage Foundation*, May 6, 2013.

> ences determined in its study of the fiscal costs of immigration, generally have to expand as new immigrants enter a community; someone has to bear the cost of that expansion.

The cost of these governmental services is far larger than many people imagine. For example, in 2010, the average U.S. household received $31,584 in government benefits and services in these four categories.

Tax Consumers

The governmental system is highly redistributive. Well-educated households tend to be *net tax contributors*: The taxes they pay exceed the direct and means-tested benefits, education, and population-based services they receive. For example, in 2010, in the whole U.S. population, households with college-educated heads, on average, received $24,839 in government benefits while paying $54,089 in taxes. The average college-educated household thus generated a fiscal surplus of $29,250 that government used to finance benefits for other households.

Many unlawful immigrants have U.S.-born children: these children are currently eligible for the full range of government welfare and medical benefits.

Other households are *net tax consumers*: The benefits they receive exceed the taxes they pay. These households generate a "fiscal deficit" that must be financed by taxes from other households or by government borrowing. For example, in 2010, in the U.S. population as a whole, households headed by persons without a high school degree, on average, received $46,582 in government benefits while paying only $11,469 in taxes. This generated an average fiscal deficit (benefits received minus taxes paid) of $35,113.

The high deficits of poorly educated households are important in the amnesty debate because the typical unlawful immigrant has only a 10th-grade education. Half of unlawful immigrant households are headed by an individual with less than a high school degree, and another 25 percent of household heads have only a high school degree.

Some argue that the deficit figures for poorly educated households in the general population are not relevant for immigrants. Many believe, for example, that lawful immigrants use little welfare. In reality, lawful immigrant households receive significantly more welfare, on average, than U.S.-born households. Overall, the fiscal deficits or surpluses for lawful immigrant households are the same as or higher than those for U.S.-born households with the same education level. Poorly educated households, whether immigrant or U.S.-born, receive far more in government benefits than they pay in taxes.

Public Education and Services

In contrast to lawful immigrants, unlawful immigrants at present do not have access to means-tested welfare, Social Security, or Medicare. This does not mean, however, that they do not receive government benefits and services. Children in unlawful immigrant households receive heavily subsidized public education. Many unlawful immigrants have U.S.-born children: these children are currently eligible for the full range of government welfare and medical benefits. And, of course, when unlawful immigrants live in a community, they use roads, parks, sewers, police, and fire protection: these services must expand to cover the added population or there will be "congestion" effects that lead to a decline in service quality.

The High Cost of Amnesty

In 2010, the average unlawful immigrant household received around $24,721 in government benefits and services while paying some $10,334 in taxes. This generated an average annual fiscal deficit (benefits received minus taxes paid) of around $14,387 per household. This cost had to be borne by U.S. taxpayers. Amnesty would provide unlawful households with access to over 80 means-tested welfare programs, Obamacare, Social Security, and Medicare. The fiscal deficit for each household would soar.

If enacted, amnesty would be implemented in phases. During the first or interim phase (which is likely to last 13 years), unlawful immigrants would be given lawful status but would be denied access to means-tested welfare and Obamacare. Most analysts assume that roughly half of unlawful immigrants work "off the books" and therefore do not pay income or FICA [Social Security] taxes. During the interim phase, these "off the books" workers would have a strong incentive to move to "on the books" employment. In addition, their wages would likely go up as they sought jobs in a more open environment. As a result, during the interim period, tax payments would rise and the average fiscal deficit among former unlawful immigrant households would fall.

After 13 years, unlawful immigrants would become eligible for means-tested welfare and Obamacare. At that point or shortly thereafter, former unlawful immigrant households would likely begin to receive government benefits at the same rate as lawful immigrant households of the same education level. As a result, government spending and fiscal deficits would increase dramatically.

The final phase of amnesty is retirement. Unlawful immigrants are not currently eligible for Social Security and Medicare, but under amnesty they would become so. The cost of this change would be very large indeed.

- As noted, at the current time (before amnesty), the average unlawful immigrant household has a net deficit (benefits received minus taxes paid) of $14,387 per household.

- During the interim phase immediately after amnesty, tax payments would increase more than government benefits, and the average fiscal deficit for former unlawful immigrant households would fall to $11,455.
- At the end of the interim period, unlawful immigrants would become eligible for means-tested welfare and medical subsidies under Obamacare. Average benefits would rise to $43,900 per household; tax payments would remain around $16,000; the average fiscal deficit (benefits minus taxes) would be about $28,000 per household.
- Amnesty would also raise retirement costs by making unlawful immigrants eligible for Social Security and Medicare, resulting in a net fiscal deficit of around $22,700 per retired amnesty recipient per year.

If amnesty is enacted, the average adult unlawful immigrant would receive $592,000 more in government benefits over the course of his remaining lifetime than he would pay in taxes.

In terms of public policy and government deficits, an important figure is the aggregate annual deficit for all unlawful immigrant households. This equals the total benefits and services received by all unlawful immigrant households minus the total taxes paid by those households.

- Under current law, all unlawful immigrant households together have an aggregate annual deficit of around $54.5 billion.
- In the interim phase (roughly the first 13 years after amnesty), the aggregate annual deficit would fall to $43.4 billion.

- At the end of the interim phase, former unlawful immigrant households would become fully eligible for means-tested welfare and health care benefits under the Affordable Care Act. The aggregate annual deficit would soar to around $106 billion.
- In the retirement phase, the annual aggregate deficit would be around $160 billion. It would slowly decline as former unlawful immigrants gradually expire.

These costs would have to be borne by already overburdened U.S. taxpayers. (All figures are in 2010 dollars.)

The typical unlawful immigrant is 34 years old. After amnesty, this individual will receive government benefits, on average, for 50 years. Restricting access to benefits for the first 13 years after amnesty therefore has only a marginal impact on long-term costs.

If amnesty is enacted, the average adult unlawful immigrant would receive $592,000 more in government benefits over the course of his remaining lifetime than he would pay in taxes.

Over a lifetime, the former unlawful immigrants together would receive $9.4 trillion in government benefits and services and pay $3.1 trillion in taxes. They would generate a lifetime fiscal deficit (total benefits minus total taxes) of $6.3 trillion. (All figures are in constant 2010 dollars.) This should be considered a minimum estimate. It probably understates real future costs because it undercounts the number of unlawful immigrants and dependents who will actually receive amnesty and underestimates significantly the future growth in welfare and medical benefits.

Misconceptions About Illegal Immigration

The debate about the fiscal consequences of unlawful and low-skill immigration is hampered by a number of misconceptions. Few lawmakers really understand the current size of government and the scope of redistribution. The fact that the average household gets $31,600 in government benefits each year is a shock. The fact that a household headed by an individual with less than a high school degree gets $46,600 is a bigger one.

Many conservatives believe that if an individual has a job and works hard, he will inevitably be a net tax contributor (paying more in taxes than he takes in benefits). In our society, this has not been true for a very long time. Similarly, many believe that unlawful immigrants work more than other groups. This is also not true. The employment rate for non-elderly adult unlawful immigrants is about the same as it is for the general population.

Many policymakers also believe that because unlawful immigrants are comparatively young, they will help relieve the fiscal strains of an aging society. Regrettably, this is not true. At every stage of the life cycle, unlawful immigrants, on average, generate fiscal deficits (benefits exceed taxes). Unlawful immigrants, on average, are always tax consumers; they never once generate a "fiscal surplus" that can be used to pay for government benefits elsewhere in society. This situation obviously will get much worse after amnesty.

Those who claim that amnesty will not create a large fiscal burden are simply in a state of denial concerning the underlying redistributional nature of government policy in the 21st century.

Many policymakers believe that after amnesty, unlawful immigrants will help make Social Security solvent. It is true that unlawful immigrants currently pay FICA taxes and would pay more after amnesty, but with average earnings of $24,800 per year, the typical unlawful immigrant will pay only about $3,700 per year in FICA taxes. After retirement, that individual is likely to draw more than $3.00 in Social Security and Medicare (adjusted for inflation) for every dollar in FICA taxes he has paid.

Moreover, taxes and benefits must be viewed holistically. It is a mistake to look at the Social Security trust fund in isolation. If an individual pays $3,700 per year into the Social Security trust fund but simultaneously draws a net $25,000 per year (benefits minus taxes) out of general government revenue, the solvency of government has not improved.

Following amnesty, the fiscal costs of former unlawful immigrant households will be roughly the same as those of lawful immigrant and non-immigrant households with the same level of education. Because U.S. government policy is highly redistributive, those costs are very large. Those who claim that amnesty will not create a large fiscal burden are simply in a state of denial concerning the underlying redistributional nature of government policy in the 21st century.

Finally, some argue that it does not matter whether unlawful immigrants create a fiscal deficit of $6.3 trillion because their children will make up for these costs. This is not true. Even if all the children of unlawful immigrants graduated from college, they would be hard-pressed to pay back $6.3 trillion in costs over their lifetimes.

Of course, not all the children of unlawful immigrants will graduate from college. Data on intergenerational social mobility show that, although the children of unlawful immigrants will have substantially better educational outcomes than their parents, these achievements will have limits. Only 13 percent are likely to graduate from college, for example. Because of this, the children, on average, are not likely to become net tax contributors. The children of unlawful immigrants are likely to remain a net fiscal burden on U.S. taxpayers, although a far smaller burden than their parents.

A final problem is that unlawful immigration appears to depress the wages of low-skill U.S.-born and lawful immigrant workers by 10 percent, or $2,300, per year. Unlawful immigration also probably drives many of our most vulnerable U.S.-born workers out of the labor force entirely. Unlawful immigration thus makes it harder for the least advantaged U.S. citizens to share in the American dream. This is wrong; public policy should support the interests of those who have a right to be here, not those who have broken our laws.

Criminal Illegal Immigrants Are a Growing Problem

Federation for American Immigration Reform

The Federation for American Immigration Reform is a nonprofit organization that seeks to improve border security, to stop illegal immigration, and to reduce immigration levels overall.

Criminal aliens—non-citizens who commit crimes—are a growing threat to public safety and national security, as well as a drain on our scarce criminal justice resources. In 1980, our federal and state prisons housed fewer than 9,000 criminal aliens. Today, about 55,000 criminal aliens account for more than one-fourth of prisoners in Federal Bureau of Prisons facilities, and there are about 297,000 criminal aliens incarcerated in state and local prisons. That number represents about 16.4 percent of the state and local prison population compared to the 12.9 percent of the total population comprised of foreign-born residents.

Administering Justice to Criminal Aliens Costs the Taxpayer Dearly

The estimated cost of incarcerating these criminal aliens at the federal level is estimated at $1.5 to $1.6 billion per year. That cost includes expenses in the federal prison system and the amount of money paid to state and local detention facilities in the State Criminal Alien Assistance Program (SCAAP). It does not include the costs of incarceration at the state and local level, nor does it include the related local costs of policing and the judicial system related to law enforcement against criminal aliens.

Our fiscal cost study in 2010, estimated administration of justice costs at the federal level related to criminal aliens at $7.8 billion annually. The comparable cost to state and local governments was $8.7 billion.

Many Criminal Aliens Are Released into Our Society to Commit Crimes Again

A Congressional Research Service report released in August 2012 found that over a 33-month period, between October 2008 and July 2011, more than 159,000 illegal aliens were arrested by local authorities and identified by the federal government as deportable but nevertheless released back onto the streets. Nearly one-sixth of those same individuals were subsequently again arrested for crimes.

Some States Bear a Disproportionate Share

Using data collected in the SCAAP system for 2009, an average share of 5.4 percent of the prisoners in state and local prisons were criminal aliens. The share was more than double that average in California (12.7%) and Arizona (11.7%). Another seven states also had criminal alien shares higher than the national average. They were: Oregon, Nevada, Colorado, Utah, New York, New Jersey, and Texas.

We must assure that the criminal conviction of an alien leads to deportation and permanent exclusion from the United States.

The shares of the incarcerated population comprised of criminal aliens are generally higher than the shares of the estimated illegal alien population in the state. For example, the estimated 2,365,000 illegal aliens in California represent 7.1 percent of the state's overall population compared to the 12.7 percent criminal alien population. Nationally, the estimated 11,920,000 illegal aliens in 2010 represented 3.9 percent of the overall population compared to the 5.4 percent criminal alien incarceration rate. This difference in shares demonstrates that the share of aliens in prison for various crimes is disproportionately large. The share of aliens in federal prisons is higher than in state and local prisons because federal prisons house aliens convicted of federal immigration offenses such as alien smuggling in addition to other crimes.

Ten states that accounted for 41 percent of the nation's total population in 2010 accounted for 63 percent of the nation's total [prison] population. Of those same states, all but Texas also have a share of the prison population that is larger than the estimated share of their illegal alien population.

What Can Be Done?

1. We must secure our borders. Denying jobs to illegal aliens through a centralized secure identity verification system is important to that effort.
2. We must assure that the criminal conviction of an alien leads to deportation and permanent exclusion from the United States.
3. Asylum applicants should be screened expeditiously and excluded if their claims are not credible. Even if they appear to have credible claims, they should be detained until background checks are done.
4. Other corrective measures include greater federal and local government cooperation to identify criminal aliens. The expansion of the Secure Communities program is useful in that regard, but it is no substitute for the 287(g) program that trains and deputizes local law enforcement personnel in immigration law enforcement.

US Legal Immigration Policies Are a Problem Too

Ann Coulter

Ann Coulter is a conservative columnist and author of the 2009 book, Guilty: Liberal Victims and Their Assault on America.

The people of Boston are no longer being terrorized by the [Boston] Marathon bombers, but amnesty supporters sure are.

On *CNN's* "State of the Union" last weekend [April 21, 2013], Sen. Lindsey Graham's response to the Boston Marathon bombers being worthless immigrants who hate America—one of whom the FBI [Federal Bureau of Investigation] cleared even after being tipped off by Russia—was to announce: "The fact that we could not track him has to be fixed."

Track him? How about not admitting him as an immigrant?

As if it's a defense, we're told Tamerlan and Dzhokhar Tsarnaev [the terrorists who set off bombs at the Boston Marathon] were disaffected "losers"—the word used by their own uncle—who couldn't make it in America. Their father had already returned to Russia. Tamerlan had dropped out of college, been arrested for domestic violence and said he had no American friends. Dzhokhar was failing most of his college courses. All of them were on welfare. . . .

My thought is, maybe we should consider admitting immigrants who can succeed in America, rather than deadbeats.

But we're not allowed to "discriminate" in favor of immigrants who would be good for America. Instead of helping

Ann Coulter, "The Problem Isn't Just Illegal Immigration, It's Legal Immigration, Too," *Townhall*, April 24, 2013.

America, our immigration policies are designed to help other countries solve their internal problems by shipping their losers to us.

Problems with Legal Immigration

The problem isn't just illegal immigration. I would rather have doctors and engineers sneaking into the country than legally arriving ditch-diggers.

Teddy Kennedy's 1965 immigration act so dramatically altered the kinds of immigrants America admits that, since 1969, about 85 percent of legal immigrants have come from the Third World. They bring Third World levels of poverty, fertility, illegitimacy and domestic violence with them. When they can't make it in America, they simply go on welfare and sometimes strike out at Americans.

During the three years from 2010 through 2012, immigrants have committed about a dozen mass murders in this country, not including the 9/11 attack.

In addition to the four dead and more than 100 badly wounded victims of the Boston Marathon bombing, let's consider a few of the many other people who would be alive, but for Kennedy's immigration law:

- The six Long Island railroad passengers murdered in 1993 by Jamaican immigrant Colin Ferguson. Before the shooting, Ferguson was unemployed, harassing women on subways, repeatedly bringing lawsuits against police and former employers, applying for workman's compensation for fake injuries and blaming all his problems on white people. Whom he then decided to murder.

- The two people killed outside CIA [Central Intelligence Agency] headquarters in 1993 by Pakistani illegal immigrant Mir Qazi. He had been working as a driver for a courier company.
- Christoffer Burmeister, a 27 year-old musician killed in a mass shooting by Palestinian immigrant Ali Hassan Abu Kamal in 1997 at the Empire State Building. Hassan had immigrated to America with his family two months earlier at age 68. (It's a smart move to bring in immigrants just in time to pay them Social Security benefits!)
- Bill Cosby's son, Ennis, killed in 1997 by 18-year-old Ukrainian immigrant Mikhail Markhasev, who had come to this country with his single mother eight years earlier—because we were running short on single mothers. Markhasev, who had a juvenile record, shot Cosby point-blank for taking too long to produce his wallet. He later bragged about killing a "ni**er."
- The three people murdered at the Appalachian School of Law in 2002 by Nigerian immigrant Peter Odighizuwa, angry at America because he had failed out of law school. At least it's understandable why our immigration policies would favor a 43-year-old law student. It's so hard to get Americans to go to law school these days!
- The stewardess and passenger murdered by Egyptian immigrant Hesham Mohamed Hadayet when he shot up the El Al ticket counter at the Los Angeles airport in 2002. Hesham, a desperately needed limousine driver, received refugee status in the U.S. because he was a member of the Muslim Brotherhood. Apparently, that's a selling point if you want to immigrate to America.

- The six men murdered by Mexican immigrant Salvador Tapia at the Windy City Core Supply warehouse in Chicago in 2003, from which he had been fired six months earlier. Tapia was still in this country despite having been arrested at least a dozen times on weapons and assault charges. Only foreign newspapers mentioned that Tapia was an immigrant. American newspapers blamed the gun.

- The six people killed in northern Wisconsin in 2004 by Hmong immigrant Chai Soua Vang, who shot his victims in the back after being caught trespassing on their property. Minnesota Public Radio later explained that Hmong hunters don't understand American laws about private property, endangered species, or really any laws written in English. It was an unusual offense for a Hmong, whose preferred crime is raping 12- to 14-year-old girls—as extensively covered in the *Fresno Bee* and *Minneapolis Star Tribune.*

- The five people murdered at the Trolley Square Shopping Mall in Salt Lake City by Bosnian immigrant Sulejman Talovic in 2007. Talovic was a Muslim high school dropout with a juvenile record. No room for you, Swedish doctor. We need resentful Muslims!

- The 32 people murdered at Virginia Tech in 2007 by Seung-Hui Cho, a South Korean immigrant.

- The 13 soldiers murdered at Fort Hood in 2009 by "accused" shooter Maj. Nidal Malik Hasan, son of Palestinian immigrants. Hasan's parents had operated a restaurant in Roanoke, Va., because where are we going to find Americans to do that?

- The 13 people killed at the American Civic Association in Binghamton, N.Y., by Vietnamese immigrant Jiverly Wong, who became a naturalized citizen two years *after* being convicted of fraud and forgery in California. Wong was angry that people disrespected him for his poor English skills.

- Florence Donovan-Gunderson, who was shot along with her husband, and three National Guardsmen in a Carson City IHOP gunned down by Mexican immigrant Eduardo Sencion in 2011.
- The three people, including a 15-year-old girl, murdered in their home in North Miami by Kesler Dufrene, a Haitian immigrant and convicted felon who had been arrested nine times, but was released when Obama halted deportations to Haiti after the earthquake. Dufrene chose the house at random.
- The many African-Americans murdered by Hispanic gangs in Los Angeles in the last few years, including Jamiel Shaw Jr., a star football player being recruited by Stanford; Cheryl Green, a 14-year-old eighth-grade student chosen for murder solely because she was black; and Christopher Ash, who witnessed Green's murder.

During the three years from 2010 through 2012, immigrants have committed about a dozen mass murders in this country, not including the 9/11 attack.

The mass murderers were from Afghanistan, South Korea, Vietnam, Haiti, South Africa, Ethiopia and Mexico. None were from Canada or Western Europe.

I don't want to hear about the black crime rate or the Columbine killers. We're talking about immigrants here! There should be ZERO immigrants committing crimes. There should be ZERO immigrants accepting government assistance. There should be ZERO immigrants demanding that we speak their language.

We have no choice about native-born losers. We ought to be able to do something about the people we chose to bring here.

Meanwhile, our government officials just keep singing the praises of "diversity," while expressly excluding skilled immigrants who might be less inclined to become "disaffected" and lash out by killing Americans.

In response to the shooting at Fort Hood, Army Chief of Staff Gen. George W. Casey Jr. said: "As horrific as this tragedy was, if our diversity becomes a casualty, I think that's worse."

On "Fox News Sunday" this week, former CIA director Gen. Michael Hayden said of the Boston bombing suspects, "We welcome these kinds of folks coming to the United States who want to be contributing American citizens."

Unless, that is, they have a college degree and bright prospects. Those immigrants are prohibited.

Illegal Immigration Benefits America

Johnny Angel Wendell

Johnny Angel Wendell is a Los Angeles-based weekly columnist and writer, musician, radio talk show host, and commercial and film actor.

Both sides of the political aisle have made a major issue out of the problem of the 11 million people inside the US illegally or presently undocumented. The president has said this is a priority and Florida senator Marco Rubio has agreed. They are theoretically opposed to each other, yet Rubio's proposals entailed in the Border Security, Economic Opportunity, and Immigration Modernization Act of 2013 don't differ a great deal from [President Barack] Obama's. In a nutshell, Rubio has suggested that the wholesale eviction of 11 million people is impossible and that the bill offers them an opportunity for legalization and permanent residence and citizenship. Naturally, the "jump through hoops" process begins here: Fines and background checks and no federal bennies.

Sounds completely reasonable, but you'd think Rubio had suggested that the government was handing out lollipops and bon-bons, making Spanish the new "official language" and changing the "Star Spangled Banner" to "Guantanmera" by the reaction of his "conservative" peers. A cursory Google reveals an enraged base represented by such intellectual heavyweights as Townhall.com and Ann "To Hell With Palin, I Was Here First" Coulter. Any concessions to the teeming masses of south of the border is treasonous amnesty and in their hardly humble opinions, this will lead to "de-Europeanization" (ie less white).

Johnny Angel Wendell, "The 'Do Nothing' Solution to 'Illegal Immigration,'" *San Francisco Bay Guardian*, May 17, 2013. www.sfbg.com.

As far as what the generally pitiful Democrats are offering, it is only marginally different than Rubio's idea. Which is also reasonable, but overlooks the crux of the issue, because no one anywhere has too unmitigated gall (until now) to say it: "Illegal Immigration reform" is a solution in search of a problem, because in reality, it isn't a problem at all!

No Aggrieved Party

The way I see it, a problem means an aggrieved party and in this instance, there isn't one. People want to hire help for whatever the task is, other people agree to do it for a price, end of story. The idea that "illegal immigrants are stealing American workers jobs" sounds fairly solid on its face unless you happen to live in the American Southwest and notice that wherever day laborers congregate, there aren't a whole hell of a lot of white folks. As far as "taking away jobs that union carpenters/plumbers/electricians do", isn't it the union's job to protect their own for one and for two, a skyscraper isn't built and wired with dudes from the Lowe's parking lot. It is not worth a major contractor's license to screw with E-Verify [a system of worker identification and verification used by some US companies] (I passed an E-verify check myself a few months ago for my radio show!).

Assuming you "legalized" every man, woman and child in the US tomorrow, what happens? The working person's price rises. Which means that they will be replaced by new people from Central America or Asia that will remain invisible. See, we are a free country with open borders—people can come and go as they please, this isn't a gulag (the irony of the most virulent anti-USSR [the former Soviet Union] voices being the loudest for a border fence is astounding). Not only is there no way to stop it, there isn't even a real reason to stop it—as China and Japan might tell you, an aging and shrinking worker base is starting to hurt them and hard.

Fact is, both major political parties support and oppose it for a pair of reasons of their own. Democrats love this, as it accelerates the "Bluing" of the Southwest with millions of new voters beholding and grateful to them, making a Republican national electoral victory mathematically impossible. The other reason they love it is because it replenishes their most loyal and organized base, labor. Republicans hate it for two reasons as well—newly legal workers will have more rights, bargaining power and higher pay, which means that a new cheap labor era is gonna take a while. The other reason is the one they vehemently deny but is as obvious as the honkers on their maps—their base's great unifier isn't economics or even social issues, but race. That the Dixiecrats of the last century are now almost entirely Republican. The glue that holds them intact, whether they'd care to admit it or not, is white supremacy. And a sea of legal Americans that are a deeper shade of soul galls them to the cores of their rancid selves. Were they serious about "sending all of these people back to where they came from", they'd boycott every and any business that employs them, which means they'd pretty much have to stop eating. I've seen what the average reactionary looks like—that ain't happening.

Undocumented workers pour billions into the coffers of state and federal [governments] . . . and whatever their costs are to health or schools, they're balanced off by what the public saves in lower food and service costs.

In fact, when the "illegals" are white, they say nothing.

Obama and Rubio both cry out that the system is "broken" but it isn't. Undocumenteds pour billions into the coffers of state and federal [governments] and don't get it back and whatever their costs are to health or schools, they're balanced off by what the public saves in lower food and service costs. They're a wash. Which means that any changes to the laissez-faire system only make everyone's life harder and more complex. If there is a solution, the easiest one would be a "seven year rule"—you prove you've actually been here 7 years, no criminal record, you take a citizenship test, that's it.

We have undocumented people in this very neighborhood. They want the same things we do. That's good enough for me.

There Is No Immigration Crisis

Kurt Schlichter

Kurt Schlichter is a successful California trial lawyer, former stand-up comic, TV commentator, and writer. He also has authored three political humor e-books.

With the immigration scam well underway in Washington [DC], the only real takeaway for the outside observer is that the Beltway [referring to the freeway surrounding the nation's capital] Establishment truly thinks we are idiots. There is no other way to explain the Establishment's tsunami of faulty premises, bogus clichés, moronic advertisements and bald-faced lies.

There is no immigration "crisis." It's not a "crisis" when people who shouldn't be here anyway don't have all the privileges of people who do have a right to be here.

That's how it *should* be.

There are a lot of people who shouldn't be here who are here, but this is a "problem," not a "crisis." They've been here for decades, since the last immigration reform fraud failed. Oddly, the solution offered by the reformers to the problem of people being here who shouldn't be here in the first place *is to let these people here who shouldn't be here stay here.*

That's like a guy going to the doctor saying he wants to lose weight and the doctor writing him a prescription for a dozen Big Macs.

Establishment Lies

All the Establishment feeds us is lies. If the reformers are so intent on securing the border, why isn't it secure right now? Why does that have to wait until we somehow let the last

Kurt Schlichter, "The Immigration 'Crisis' Is No Crisis," Townhall.com, June 13, 2013.

bunch of people who scoffed at our sovereignty get on their pathway to citizenship before we take the most basic step any nation must take to be a nation at all—to protect our borders?

The answer is simple—they don't *want* to secure the border, they never have wanted to secure the border, and they never will secure the border, at least until forced to do so, and then only grudgingly and while employing every passive aggressive tool they can to subvert doing so.

And they'll even tell you they have no intention of securing the border—provided you speak Spanish.

To convince us of the vital need to immediately, this minute, right now, no time to think about it, pass their thousand-page wish list of immigration giveaways we get clichés. Facts? Numbers? No, we get told we must do it because illegals need to "come out of the shadows."

[Amnesty for illegal immigrants] will help crony corporatists who want a docile, dirt-cheap labor force. But what's in it for us regular people?

The hell they do. If you shouldn't be here you *should* be in the shadows.

We get told that bringing in some untold millions of low-skill immigrants—*30 million* or more—will "help our economy." Let's assume that's true. Let's even assume what we all know is a lie, that none of these people will be able to cash in on the welfare state that already pays too much money to freeloaders who have a right to be here.

So how much money, in dollars, will this bounty bring each of us? I know it will help crony corporatists who want a docile, dirt-cheap labor force. But what's in it for us regular people?

That's a legitimate question, and I've never heard the straight answer we deserve. After all, this is my country, and adding a zillion new voters will dilute my voting rights, so I'm giving up something. What I am giving up is really, really valuable to me—American citizenship.

I may have been lucky enough to be born into my citizenship, but I *earned* it in two wars. And my wife and her family—who respected the United States enough to ask for permission to become citizens and then either served in uniform or saw-off family members to war to defend her—*earned* it too.

So, when we ask why we should just give citizenship away to people who have already disrespected us by coming here uninvited, we deserve an answer, and not some cliché or vague platitude either. If this is going to benefit us, we want to know exactly how, and how much. Then we'll know if it's also in *our* best interest to do it.

But we won't get an answer. The fact is that this is not meant to benefit *us*. It's meant to benefit the Establishment. We just get to pick up the tab.

"Trust us," they say. The IRS [Internal Revenue Service], the NSA [National Security Administration], reporter subpoenas, Fast and Furious, Benghazi, Obamacare: I'm done trusting the Establishment.

Citizenship for Future Democratic Voters

So we get those ubiquitous advertisements on conservative shows to try and fool us into signing on. The one from the weirdly-named, liberal front group "Americans for a Conservative Direction" offers the usual lies about securing the border first. They think they can distract us from the prize—citizenship for millions of future Democrat voters.

Why again am I morally obligated to allow a bunch of people who shouldn't be here in the first place to vote when I know, and you know, and everyone knows, they will vote *en masse* for my political opponents?

I wish the GOP [Grand Old Party, a nickname for Republicans] Establishment was as intent on destroying liberalism as it seems to be on destroying conservatism.

Maybe "comprehensive reform" is what Jesus commands in some chapter of the New Testament that none of my ministers have ever mentioned, perhaps the Book of Mario or the Gospel According to Chuck. That's the message of the most obnoxious ad, the one that assumes Christian conservatives are morons who will fall for anything pushed by a quivering-voiced "evangelical" babbling about prayers. This simpering woman sounds like she's about to burst into tears as she asserts that Christ commands us to give away the store to the illegals.

Maybe in your Bible, lady, but not mine.

I'd be insulted that the people behind these cheesy ploys think we are that dumb, except those coastal enclave Establishment types know nothing about us at all. Well, except for one thing—they know that *we* are the only obstacle to them pushing through this obnoxious, ruinous disaster.

They are scared of us, because they know that our representatives fear us and our votes more than they fear the Establishment. So they lie to us, try to rush through their scheme, and trick us into just letting it happen.

There is no immigration "crisis." The only "crisis" is the one faced by an Establishment that needs millions of new voters to cling to power because millions of real Americans are waking up to the nightmare they have created.

Illegal Immigrants Are Really Guest Workers. We Just Pretend Otherwise

Eric Posner

*Eric Posner is a professor at the University of Chicago Law School and coauthor of two books—*The Executive Unbound: After the Madisonian Republic *(2011) and* Climate Change Justice *(2010).*

The United States has a well-functioning system of guest workers, whether or not it's enshrined in law.

An estimated 11 million people live in the United States illegally. Everyone agrees that this is intolerable, and—deportation being impossible and possibly unfair—Congress appears on the verge of granting them a path to citizenship. But legal reform is not going to solve the problem of illegal immigration. That's because illegal immigration is not really a problem, or if it is a problem, it is a problem that no one wants to solve.

A De Facto Guest Worker Program

It is common to think that the huge pool of illegal immigrants reflects a failure of government. Congress has established rules that determine who gets in and who stays out, but has failed to spend the money to enforce the law. The solution is more enforcement resources, symbolized by the huge wall being constructed among the Saguaros in the Sonoran desert.

Eric Posner, "Illegal Immigrants Are Really Guest Workers. We Just Pretend Otherwise," *Slate*, February 4, 2013.

But the reality is that the United States has long been well served by a three-tiered system of immigration. The top tier consists of highly desired foreign workers, who are offered green cards, which typically lead to citizenship. The second tier consists of skilled and semi-skilled people who can obtain short-term visas, usually for three years. Some of them prove themselves while here, and end up acquiring a green card as well. Then there is a third tier, typically unskilled people, who can be removed at any time and for any reason, yet are frequently permitted certain privileges, such as a driver's license. They are also permitted to work—while in practice being denied the protection of employment and labor laws. We call these people "illegal immigrants" but that is a misnomer. Little effort is made to stop them from working or to expel them. And those who proved themselves by staying employed, learning English, and making enough money to afford a moderate fine, were given a path to citizenship in 1986, as may occur again if Congress passes immigration reform this year.

What we have is a de facto quasi-guest-worker system, where foreign workers . . . are permitted to stay and work as long as they do not commit a serious crime, look like terrorists, or cause other trouble.

Illegal immigrants do break the law, but they break the law in the sense that everyone breaks the law. Think of traffic laws, which everyone breaks but which are also only enforced selectively—largely against people suspected of committing drug crimes or other misdeeds. The law against illegal entry is (sort of) enforced at the border, but hardly at all against people once they arrive, except if they commit serious crimes, in which case they are sent to jail and then deported.

It is an open secret that illegal workers are, or have been, employed by some of the country's largest and most important companies, like Tyson Foods. Yet the number of worksite enforcement actions—where federal immigration authorities raid a worksite and drag away illegal workers—has been minuscule. In 2011, worksite raids resulted in the arrest of 1,471 illegal workers out of an estimated 8 million. In the same year, only 385 employers out of 6 million were fined for hiring illegal workers. And this counted for an increase from 2006, when precisely zero employers were punished. In other words, the odds of being punished for participating in the illegal immigration economy are something like the odds of being given a ticket for driving 56 mph in a 55 mph zone. Despite the federal system E-Verify [a voluntary system of worker verification], efforts to force employers to check the status of job applicants have mostly foundered because of their cost and the risk that lawful residents will be mistakenly deemed illegal (though this is in fact rare). Which is just to say that we are unwilling to incur the enforcement costs because we don't actually want to enforce.

What we have is a de facto quasi-guest-worker system, where foreign workers who overstay their visas or sneak across the border are permitted to stay and work as long as they do not commit a serious crime, look like terrorists, or cause other trouble. In many places, authorities take pains to assure illegal immigrants that they will not be turned over to federal Immigration and Customs Enforcement so that they will cooperate with the police and social services. Anxious to attract new residents, Baltimore, for example, prohibits its employees, including police, from asking anyone about his or her immigration status. Of course, Arizona, which has suffered from violent crime associated with border crossings, has tried to crack down, but it is an exception.

Serving American Interests

The system exists because it serves America's interests. Americans have a voracious appetite for unskilled labor—in the form of nannies, gardeners, restaurant workers, agricultural laborers, construction workers, and factory hands. And foreign countries contain huge pools of unskilled labor. Unskilled Mexican laborers would rather pick strawberries in the United States for a pittance than pick strawberries in Mexico that are exported to the United States, and for which they are paid even less than a pittance. U.S. businesses would rather pay illegal workers a pittance than Americans a pittance and a half.

What is ingenious about our system is that it allows us to take advantage of unskilled labor at low cost; exile those people who cause trouble; and ultimately grant amnesty to those who prove their worth by working steadily, learning English, and obeying criminal law. They will leave on their own when unemployment rises, and come back when labor is in demand. In this way public policy recognizes a sliding scale of legal protections for aliens, offering the strongest protections to those we want the most, and the weakest protections to those we are less sure about.

Why not recognize this guest-worker system in law? The bipartisan framework for immigration reform hints at such a change without explicitly endorsing it. But others have proposed this, and it was seriously considered in 2007 immigration reform negotiations.

The idea of making our guest-worker system official is to move potential illegal workers into legal channels, where they can be tracked and also protected from exploitation. Liberals have long opposed any system that creates second-class citizens, but because liberals also oppose harsh immigration enforcement measures, they end up reaping the benefits of a pool of low-wage second-class citizens without calling them that. Unions oppose guest-worker programs because union organization requires a long-term commitment, which temporary workers cannot make, while they compete with union members for jobs.

But these are not the real obstacles to a guest-worker program. Enshrined in law, such a system could solve the problem of illegal immigration only if it authorized the same low wages and bad working conditions that illegal workers currently accept. The demand for such workers is so high precisely because they lack legal protections, and can be paid little and often treated poorly. The more generous the guest-worker program is, the more likely that it will be evaded. At the same time, however, neither Republicans nor Democrats will support a guest-worker program that permits foreign workers to be paid less than the minimum wage. And guest workers, like illegal immigrants, integrate themselves here and have children who become American citizens. It would be difficult to demand or force them to leave if they do not want to. In the end, they are not really guests.

Here's a prediction. A path to citizenship will be offered to the current 11 million, and if it is not too onerous, most of them will take it. But others will not, planting the seeds of a new illegal population. Possibly a guest-worker program will be put into place, but even if so, it will be too small and too entangled with bureaucracy for employers and workers to want to use. Over the years, millions more people from Mexico and especially (as Mexico's economy continues to improve) Central and South America will illegally enter the United States. They will be partly drawn by jobs, and partly by waiting family and friends, and the law will not deter them because they expect that sooner or later another path to citizenship will open up. Ten or 20 years from now, everyone will recognize a new illegal immigration "problem," which we will again "solve" by removing the "illegal" label from the foreheads of the migrants and affixing the "legal" label in its place.

CHAPTER 2

Does the US Government Adequately Enforce Immigration Laws?

Chapter Preface

The United States shares a border with Mexico that stretches two thousand miles—all the way from the southern tip of Texas to California—and preventing illegal crossings of this border is a significant part of the US immigration enforcement system. The nation also shares a long border with Canada that must be monitored, but the southern border presents a much greater threat of illegal immigration. Border security involves a staff of thousands of Border Patrol agents, hundreds of miles of border fencing, management of numerous land ports of entry, technological surveillance efforts, and various other operations to disrupt criminal and drug organizations and maintain peaceful border cities. President Barack Obama claims to have strengthened security at the US borders, but his conservative critics assert that much more needs to be done, and this has become one of the points of contention in the current immigration reform debate.

According to President Obama, his administration has doubled the number of Border Patrol agents from about ten thousand in 2004 to more than twenty-one thousand in 2011, creating the largest Border Patrol presence on the southern border in the nation's history. President Obama also has sent unmanned drones to do aerial surveillance along the southern border, assisting personnel on the ground. The White House also claims that the Department of Homeland Security (DHS), the country's immigration agency, has competed 649 miles of new fencing along the Mexico border, while at the same time focusing Immigration and Customs Enforcement (ICE) agents—DHS's investigative arm—on disrupting criminal organizations and cartels involved in drug smuggling and gun trafficking that contribute to violence on the border.

These efforts, the administration says, have helped reduce the number of illegal crossings by 80 percent from their peak in 2000. The White House website notes that apprehensions of illegal border crossers have decreased 53 percent just since 2008—from about 724,000 in 2008 to approximately 340,000 in 2011. And in the last two and a half years, DHS reportedly has seized 75 percent more cash, 31 percent more drugs, and 64 percent more weapons along the southwest border compared to the previous two and a half years. The administration also touts the low crime rates of border cities such as San Diego, Phoenix, and El Paso and says it is working closely with Mexico and Canada to enhance security and trade, while improving the more than thirty-five ports of entry with new technology such as thermal camera systems, mobile surveillance, and remote video surveillance.

Administration critics, however, say the border security picture is not quite as bright as the president suggests. Many commentators note that the decrease in apprehensions is at least partly due to the US recession, which has discouraged people from coming to the United States to find jobs. In addition, critics say that it is very difficult to measure border control success because there is no reliable way to count the number of people who successfully crossed the border illegally and avoided being caught. Neither does the government have a good way to determine which border security measures (such as fences, agents, cameras, or drones) are most effective. Although Republicans typically demand, and the Congress has repeatedly awarded, more funding to border security, many observers say there is really no clear evidence that more money means more effective border security. Large amounts of border security funding have in the past gone to programs that ultimately were abandoned: one example is a virtual fence project supported by former president George W. Bush.

Yet the Senate proposal for immigration reform once again calls for increased spending on border enforcement. Sponsors of the Senate legislation added provisions to the bill to fund twenty-one thousand new Border Patrol agents and seven hundred miles of new fencing—at a cost of about $25 billion—in order to secure enough Republican votes to pass the legislation in the Senate. The Congressional Budget Office (CBO), a federal agency that provides fiscal advice to Congress, concluded that this reform could reduce illegal border crossings by one-third to one-half. Not everyone agrees that this is a cost-effective policy, however. Some immigration reform experts argue that spending this much money to reduce apprehensions when border crossings are already at a record low is foolish. Directing such large amounts of money to add more Border Patrol agents, some critics say, is also not a wise idea when other improvements would be more useful, such as improving ports of entry or providing better training and equipment for existing personnel.

The authors of viewpoints included in this chapter of *Current Controversies: Immigration* delve into various other parts of the US immigration enforcement system and discuss whether these enforcement efforts are adequate.

Immigration Laws Are Enforced Now More than Ever

Immigration Policy Center

The Immigration Policy Center is the research and policy arm of the American Immigration Council, a nonprofit organization that honors America's immigrant history and seeks to shape rational immigration policies.

With roughly 11 million unauthorized immigrants living in the United States, some question whether the nation's immigration laws are being seriously enforced. In truth, due to legal and policy changes in recent years, the immigration laws are enforced more strictly now than ever before. The Department of Homeland Security (DHS) has reported record numbers of removals during the [Barack] Obama administration, especially of noncitizens with criminal convictions. Meanwhile, fewer noncitizens are trying to enter the country illegally, and those caught by the Border Patrol are now regularly charged with federal crimes. Together, these trends reflect a sweeping and punitive transformation in U.S. immigration enforcement.

"Removals" and "Returns"

When noncitizens who violate the immigration laws are forced to leave the United States, their departure is classified as a "removal" or a "return." [A removal is where the noncitizen leaves the United States based on an order of removal, or deportation. A return is when the noncitizen leaves the country not based on a deportation order.] DHS reported 391,953 "removals" during the 2011 fiscal year, slightly below the record set in 2009. Meanwhile, DHS reported 323,542 "returns" in 2011, the lowest number since 1970.

Both figures continue a trend in which the number of "removals" has steadily risen while the number of "returns" has drastically fallen. This trend is important because it reflects a significant change in apprehension patterns. While "returns" generally occur along the border, "removals" typically involve noncitizens already residing in the United States. Thus, the rising number of "removals" and falling number of "returns" suggests that more noncitizens are now being deported from the country than are caught trying to enter illegally in the first place.

The total number of "removals" and "returns" reported by DHS should not be confused with those reported by U.S. Immigration and Customs Enforcement (ICE), an agency within DHS. In fiscal 2011, ICE reported 319,077 "removals," a record for the agency.

Accounting for These Trends

With regard to DHS as a whole, there are at least three overlapping explanations why the annual number of "returns" has fallen for much of the last decade while the number of "removals" has risen. First, as previously noted, noncitizens caught crossing the border are generally "returned" rather than "removed," and the Border Patrol has made fewer "apprehensions" (i.e. arrests) in each of the last seven fiscal years. In fiscal 2011, the number of apprehensions (340,252) made by Border Patrol agents represented a 27 percent decrease from 2010 and the lowest total in 40 years.

Second, through the expansion of the Secure Communities program, ICE is now able to cross-check the fingerprints of persons arrested by state and local police against those in its own databases. For example, in July 2009, when Secure Communities had been deployed in fewer than 80 jurisdictions, the program resulted in fewer than 12,000 fingerprint matches. In July 2012, when Secure Communities was active in more than 3,000 jurisdictions, the program resulted in nearly 44,000 fingerprint matches.

In recent years . . . a growing number of noncitizens have been charged in federal criminal courts for illegally entering the country.

Finally, changes to U.S. immigration laws enacted in 1996 permit DHS to "remove" many noncitizens without holding a hearing before an immigration judge. Under certain circumstances, for example, noncitizens may receive "expedited removal orders" and "reinstatements of removal" without having to appear in court. Indeed, the rise in "removals" over the past decade is largely due to an increase in removal orders issued by DHS officers rather than immigration judges.

"Criminal" and "Noncriminal" Removals

In recent years, DHS has attempted to prioritize the removal of "criminals" over "noncriminals." According to DHS, noncitizens are considered "criminal" if they have ever been convicted of a crime, no matter how minor. During the 2011 fiscal year, 188,832 removals (48.1 percent) involved noncitizens who had a criminal conviction—the highest number in the last decade. Meanwhile, 203,571 removals (51.9 percent) involved noncitizens with no criminal conviction—the lowest number in five years.

Since fiscal 2009, the most frequent types of criminal convictions for noncitizens removed from the United States involved drug, traffic, and immigration offenses. In 2011, the government removed 43,262 noncitizens convicted of drug offenses, 43,022 noncitizens convicted of traffic offenses, and 37,458 noncitizens convicted of immigration offenses. As noted below, however, many of those charged with immigration offenses might just as easily have been prosecuted civilly, rendering increases in "criminal" prosecutions in this category somewhat misleading.

"Illegal Entry" and "Illegal Re-entry"

Most noncitizens charged with violating the immigration laws are removed or returned but not criminally prosecuted. In recent years, however, a growing number of noncitizens have been charged in federal criminal courts for illegally entering the country.

The rise in criminal immigration prosecutions is largely traceable to "Operation Streamline," an effort launched during the Bush administration to bring criminal charges against noncitizens apprehended by the Border Patrol. Noncitizens prosecuted under Operation Streamline are typically charged with "illegal entry" and/or "illegal re-entry." Illegal entry, which occurs any time a noncitizen enters the country in violation of the law, is a federal misdemeanor punishable by up to 180 days in prison. Illegal re-entry, which occurs when a noncitizen unlawfully returns after a prior order of removal, is a federal felony punishable by up to two years in prison.

In fiscal 2010, the most recent year for which figures are available, the Justice Department brought charges of illegal entry in 43,300 cases and illegal re-entry in 35,390 cases. The number of charges for illegal entry represented a slight decline from prior fiscal years, while the number of illegal re-entry charges marked the highest figure in U.S. history.

A Transformation in Immigration Enforcement

Over the past decade, immigration enforcement has undergone a fundamental transformation in the United States. Due to changes to the immigration laws and the expansion of the Secure Communities program, more noncitizens are being "removed" than ever before—making it more difficult for them to return legally to the United States and exposing them to felony charges if they re-enter the country illegally. Meanwhile, the number of apprehensions along the border has fallen to levels not seen since the early 1970s, and the government now regularly prosecutes noncitizens for illegally entering and re-entering the country. In combination, these trends demonstrate that the immigration laws are being more strictly enforced today than ever before.

President Barack Obama Has Merely Shifted Priorities in Immigration Enforcement

PolitiFact.com

PolitiFact.com is a website and project of the Tampa Bay Times *that examines and researches political statements to rate their truth or falsehood.*

Republican Sen. Marco Rubio is taking a precarious lead on immigration reform within his party, where the vocal conservative wing is wary of any hint of amnesty for people living in the U.S. illegally.

Rubio is framing his case, in part, by reminding Republicans that they don't want President Barack Obama leading the way on this issue.

"We are dealing with 11 million people, but we are also dealing with the future of immigration in this country, and we are dealing with an administration that, quite frankly, has shown a reluctance to enforce the immigration law," Rubio told *Fox News*' Greta Van Susteren on April 30, 2013. "Look, if you want to know the single impediment to get things done . . . people don't believe the Obama administration or the federal government will enforce the law."

As Rubio continues barnstorming for immigration reform, the claim that Obama has gone soft on enforcement has become part of his script.

Is it true?

We reached out to Rubio's spokesman, Alex Conant, the White House and other experts to evaluate Obama's record on enforcing immigration law.

First, we'll examine points from Obama's critics, evidence that they say shows he is reluctant to enforce immigration law. Then we'll look at the other side, at evidence that some say shows Obama has vigorously enforced immigration law.

Where Enforcement Has Decreased

Prosecutorial discretion on deportations. Conant pointed us to the criticism that the Obama administration is choosing not to deport millions of known illegal immigrants.

In 2011, the administration announced a policy of making deportation of criminals (think violent offenders, gang members and drug traffickers) who are in the U.S. illegally a top priority. Those with no criminal record or threat to public safety became a low priority and would likely be allowed to remain in the U.S.

These positions are enshrined in the "Morton memos," directives from U.S. Immigration and Customs Enforcement [ICE] Director John Morton issued in June 2011.

In June 2012, Obama announced that his administration would no longer deport young undocumented immigrants if they met certain criteria, including having entered the United States as children, having a clean criminal record and attending school.

"ICE . . . has limited resources to remove those illegally in the United States. ICE must prioritize the use of its enforcement personnel, detention space and removal assets to ensure that the aliens it removes represent, as much as reasonably possible, the agency's enforcement priorities, namely the promotion of national security, border security, public safety, and the integrity of the immigration system," Morton wrote.

That meant that family members, students and other long-time resident immigrants would not be targeted.

Deferred action on immigrants brought as children. Conant also cited Obama's actions on immigrants who were brought to the United States illegally as children, commonly called "Dreamers."

In June 2012, Obama announced that his administration would no longer deport young undocumented immigrants if they met certain criteria, including having entered the United States as children, having a clean criminal record and attending school.

Prosecutorial discretion and deferred action no doubt mean that certain segments of immigrants are not being eyed for deportation. But David Martin, an international law professor at the University of Virginia School of Law, argued that doesn't add up to a reluctance to enforce the law. He said it's "choosing different things to enforce."

"There's been an effort since very early to be more serious and more systematic about the priorities," Martin said. "In my view that's a perfectly appropriately way to operate a law enforcement agency. I see it as more sensible enforcement."

Position on "border triggers." Many Republicans, including Rubio, want immigration reform to include a "trigger" that says the border will be secure before immigrants can begin the path toward legal status or citizenship. The Obama administration opposes such a trigger.

"I think that once people really look at the whole system and how it works, relying on one thing as a so-called trigger is not the way to go," Homeland Security Secretary Janet Napolitano said in March 2013. "There needs to be certainty in the bill so that people know when they can legalize and then when the pathway to citizenship, earned citizenship, would open up."

A border trigger, however, is a mechanism of proposed law—not something currently in place that the Obama administration is declining to enforce.

A lawsuit against Arizona. Is Obama not only shying from enforcement, but also going after states that are getting tough?

Conant noted the Justice Department's 2010 lawsuit against the state of Arizona over its controversial immigration law that grants local police greater authority to check the legal status of people they stop. The law was meant to "discourage and deter" illegal immigrants from staying in the state.

Federal officials said Arizona's law would flood them with cases of illegal immigrants who pose no danger.

But the federal government's lawsuit is a constitutional issue more than an enforcement one.

"They went after Arizona on a constitutional principle that the federal government is in charge of immigration and it's the federal government that should be making immigration laws, not Arizona," said Stephen Yale-Loehr, an immigration attorney and adjunct professor at Cornell Law School.

No more 287(g) program. Jessica Zuckerman, a homeland security analyst for the conservative Heritage Foundation, said the Obama administration has "all but abolished" a program that allows state and local law enforcement to essentially be deputized as immigration agents and be allowed to arrest people for immigration issues. It's known as 287(g).

"That program's been undercut basically to the point that it doesn't exist anymore," Zuckerman said.

Large-scale workplace arrests of illegal workers were hallmarks of the George W. Bush administration's approach, and in 2011 arrests from worksite raids had dropped by 70 percent since Bush left office.

Indeed, this 2012 announcement from Immigration and Customs Enforcement, or ICE, says exactly that.

"ICE has also decided not to renew any of its agreements with state and local law enforcement agencies that operate task forces under the 287(g) program. ICE has concluded that other enforcement programs . . . are a more efficient use of resources for focusing on priority cases," the announcement said.

Fewer workplace raids. Zuckerman also said far fewer random searches are occurring at workplaces where illegal immigrants are suspected to be employed.

Large-scale workplace arrests of illegal workers were hallmarks of the George W. Bush administration's approach, and in 2011 arrests from worksite raids had dropped by 70 percent since Bush left office.

That too reflected Obama's contrasting priorities, as ICE officials turned their attention to employers. If immigration inspectors found evidence that immigrant workers' identity documents might be false, managers had to dismiss the workers or risk prosecution.

But Zuckerman argues that document audits don't equal enforcement.

"It needs to be part of other enforcement measures that have decreased," she said. "None of them alone is a silver bullet."

Overall deportations of illegal immigrants have increased during Obama's term.

Where Enforcement Has Increased

Experts also told us that Obama has ramped up enforcement on some avenues of immigration law.

"*Secure Communities.*" While backing away from the 287(g) program, the Obama administration put renewed emphasis on the Secure Communities program which is meant to identify "dangerous criminal aliens" for deportation. Local law enforcement agencies send criminal suspects' fingerprints to be checked in national crime databases. If an arrestee turns out to be an illegal immigrant with a serious rap sheet, the person can be taken into federal custody.

Alex Nowrasteh, an immigration policy analyst with the libertarian Cato Institute, said the program was used in about 3 percent of U.S. jurisdictions when Obama took office and is in about 97 percent today.

Secure Communities, he said, "is the most effective immigration enforcement tool to date as it conscripts local law enforcement into enforcing federal immigration laws.

Zuckerman, however, noted that "it only focuses on criminal aliens and not the broader issue."

Deportations are up. It has been widely reported that overall deportations of illegal immigrants have increased during Obama's term.

ICE deported 409,949 immigrants in the 2012 fiscal year, up from 396,096 immigrants in FY 2011 and more than 392,000 immigrants in FY 2010. Those figures all show a steady increase over every year of the Bush administration. . . .

Those numbers, however, are disputed by critics who note that deportations at the border are up, while other types—such as those from the defunct 287(g) program—have dropped off.

While fewer workplace raids are happening, the Obama administration is focusing more on prosecutions against employers and doing more audits of workers' documentation paperwork.

"They're doing a different kind of enforcement that results in higher numbers, but there are definitely not more people being removed from the interior of the country," Jessica Vaughan, director of policy studies at the Center for Immigration Studies which favors lower immigration levels, told the *Washington Times* recently.

At PolitiFact, we have also noted that personnel and other resources to stop illegal crossings at the U.S.-Mexico border have increased dramatically in recent years. The number of border patrol officers more than doubled from about 10,000 to about 21,000 between 2004 and 2012.

Employer prosecutions. As we noted above, while fewer workplace raids are happening, the Obama administration is focusing more on prosecutions against employers and doing more audits of workers' documentation paperwork to ensure immigration compliance.

In 2011, the *New York Times* reported that ICE started 2,746 workplace investigations, more than double the number in 2008. Fines totaling a record $43 million were levied on companies in immigration cases.

Our Ruling

Rubio said the Obama administration "has shown a reluctance to enforce the immigration law."

His spokesman pointed out some concrete changes in how Obama has approached immigration, namely a program to allow people brought here illegally as children to seek deferred action on deportation and an emphasis on deporting criminals while leaving many illegal residents who are otherwise law abiders alone. But while Rubio calls that reluctance, others see it as prioritizing. Obama has put new emphasis on some approaches, such as adding border agents, while minimizing others, such as the 287(g) program.

Whether those priorities represent sound policy is a matter of opinion. But Rubio's statement suggests that Obama has turned his back on enforcing the law, and the reality is much more nuanced than that. We rate the statement Half True.

President Barack Obama Has Dismantled US Immigration Enforcement Laws

Bob Dane and Kristen Williamson

Bob Dane is the communications director of the Federation for American Immigration Reform (FAIR), a nonprofit group that seeks to stop illegal immigration. Kristen Williamson is press secretary for FAIR.

The ancient Chinese practice of *lingchi*, the "Death of a Thousand Cuts," best describes the manner in which the [Barack] Obama administration has systematically whittled away most immigration enforcement since taking office. Over time, the rule of law has been shredded not by a single act, but by many small cuts.

A review of President Obama's record reveals a jaw-dropping steady and stealthy dismantling of virtually every tool and resource used to identify and remove deportable aliens.

Out with the Old—Gut What Works

Immediately after taking office, the Obama administration replaced effective worksite enforcement that targeted both employers and illegal workers with meaningless paper audits and modest fines. Meanwhile, the administration refused to consider making E-Verify [a program for electronic worker identification] mandatory for all employers, even resisting efforts to permanently reauthorize it, despite hundreds of thousands of businesses voluntarily using the program.

Failing to hold employers who hire illegal aliens accountable was an early, yet clear signal that the Obama administration intended to derail all enforcement.

The administration focused their sights next on programs that helped local law enforcement identify illegal aliens. Both the 287(g) and the Secure Communities agreements were rewritten to emphasize that only criminal aliens would be processed. A "don't-ask, don't-tell" policy took effect for all other illegal aliens.

In with the New—Rewrite the Rules

In 2011, Obama's Immigration and Customs Enforcement (ICE) Director, John Morton, issued a series of internal directives instructing agency staff to focus their efforts exclusively on removing illegal aliens with criminal records. The administration would exercise "prosecutorial discretion" for all others. The new priorities—still in place—imply that immigration violations, in and of themselves, are inconsequential.

While deportations for violent criminal aliens had risen, all other deportations were down indicating that the Obama administration felt it could pick and choose which laws to enforce.

Squash Resistance—Sue the States

With local programs such as 287(g) and Secure Communities weakened and federal authority (to not enforce the law) broadened by way of the new internal memos, the administration had consolidated the power it needed to initiate backdoor amnesty without interference. Attorney General Eric Holder's Department of Justice (DOJ) became the instrument of intimidation. States that enacted their own bills requiring local police to identify illegal aliens and turn them over to federal custody, felt the blows one after the other. The DOJ sued Arizona, South Carolina, and Utah.

Distract and Deceive

To distract attention from his actions, Obama told Americans that the border was secure and that that deportations were up.

Both were deceptions.

In official documents, DHS [Department of Homeland Security] stated that only 44% of the border was under operational control. And while deportations had, in fact risen slightly, the increase had nothing to do with expanding enforcement by the Obama administration. A "pipeline" of deportable cases was filled by vigorous enforcement during the last two years of the Bush administration. Those cases carried forward and Obama took credit in his first two years. Moreover, while deportations for violent criminal aliens had risen, all other deportations were down indicating that the Obama administration felt it could pick and choose which laws to enforce.

The Final Blow

From the beginning, President Obama knew that the public would reject amnesty legislation. However, he also knew he stood a good chance of getting it done through a strategy of piecemeal efforts, provided no one noticed.

With an election looming and special interests demanding grandiose and immediate action, in June [2012] President Obama declared unilaterally that he was using executive power to implement the DREAM Act for an untold number illegal alien "kids" who were brought here through "no fault of their own."

During his DREAM Act speech, Obama failed to mention that his new edict allowed illegal aliens up to the age of 30 to qualify.

Then, in an interview shortly thereafter with *CNN*'s Wolf Blitzer, DHS Secretary [Janet] Napolitano admitted that parents of illegal aliens applying for deferred action—illegal alien adults who most certainly did knowingly break the law—will not be subject to immigration enforcement. As she said, "we have it internally set up."

With that announcement, amnesty for illegal aliens tripled.

So much for Obama's argument he was giving amnesty just to "kids" who were "brought here through no fault of their own."

Obama's Death of a Thousand Cuts has virtually gutted our country's immigration enforcement apparatus, but the record is clear and the public must hold this president accountable. Congress has an urgent mandate to begin the work of restoring credibility to our immigration system by stopping the cuts, healing the wounds, and reinstating the rule of law.

President Barack Obama's Deferred Action Program Has Weakened Immigration Enforcement

Jessica Vaughan

Jessica Vaughan is director of policy studies for the Center for Immigration Studies, a nonprofit research organization that provides information about the consequences of legal and illegal immigration into the United States.

On April 8, [2013] a federal judge in Dallas heard arguments in *Crane v Napolitano*, the lawsuit brought by 10 ICE [Immigration and Customs Enforcement] officers challenging the Obama administration's Deferred Action program (DACA) and "prosecutorial discretion" policies. The hearing, at which two ICE agents and I testified, produced new information on some little-publicized side effects of the amnesty policy, including how criminal aliens have been shielded from removal. My testimony focused on internal DHS [Department of Homeland Security] statistics showing a significant decline in the number of deportations, interior enforcement, and even criminal alien removals following the implementation of these policies. I also described how the administration has cooked its removal statistics in a way that gives lawmakers and the public the false impression that enforcement has improved.

The hearing took place on the 11th floor of a federal office building in Dallas. In attendance were: Judge Reed O'Connor; [ICE officers] Kris Kobach and Michael Jung; counsel for the ICE officers; their three witnesses; four Department

Jessica Vaughan, "Lawsuit Documents Criminal Alien Releases, Decline in Enforcement, Cooked Statistics," *Center for Immigration Studies*, April 9, 2013.

of Justice lawyers representing the defendant, DHS Secretary Janet Napolitano; two local ICE lawyers assisting them; two unidentified members of the DOJ [Department of Justice] defense team; and a handful of local reporters and courtroom staff.

Releasing Illegal Aliens

The first witness called was Chris Crane, president of the ICE Officers' union. He articulated the union's view that the DACA program and the administration's "prosecutorial discretion" policies are illegal and put officers in the untenable position of releasing illegal aliens from custody who have been identified as a result of criminal behavior, simply because they claim to qualify for DACA. He said that asking for deferred action is the latest fad in jailhouses with large numbers of illegal alien inmates because word has gotten around that ICE agents are required to take these claims at face value, without verification, and will release them instead of putting them on the path to removal. Crane testified that agents hear and observe inmates advising each other on what to say. He also stated that in many cases of claimed DACA eligibility, ICE officers do not create a record of the encounter and instead delete the file so that these cases do not remain in the system for future reference.

Crane described how just last week, an alien who, within 48 hours of getting approved for deferred action by USCIS (following a prior arrest), was again arrested by local police for cocaine distribution.

The second witness was ICE officer Sam Martin, who is assigned to the Criminal Alien Program in El Paso, Texas. Martin's job is to review records that are transmitted electronically to ICE from the El Paso County jail, and determine if any of the alien inmates are removable. He testified that since the implementation of DACA, he and other ICE agents are releasing a significant number of illegal alien criminals—about 25 percent of his caseload—back to the streets.

Contrary to the administration's claims that they have achieved record levels of enforcement, the number of removals [of criminal aliens] is now 40 percent lower than ... in June 2011.

Martin said that, typically, as soon as officers inform illegal alien inmates that they will be placed in removal proceedings and read them their rights, inmates will promptly chirp up that they are eligible for what they all call "Obama's Dream Act". He confirmed that the officers are obligated to accept the claim and release the alien.

The defense team claimed that the DACA policy gives field officers leeway to screen out dangerous aliens, but apparently at least one ICE supervisor hasn't gotten the memo. Martin testified that on July 17, 2012, he went to the El Paso jail with a partner to interview an alien who had been arrested for aggravated assault on a family member and obstructing a call to 911. The alien admitted he was here illegally, and when the officers escorted him to the car for transfer to ICE detention, he attempted to escape and then, as they pursued him, he assaulted the officers, committing a series of felonies. When they arrived at the ICE processing center and started to prepare the removal paperwork, their supervisor intervened and ordered them to release the alien because he qualified for DACA. Martin is still recovering from his injuries. No further charges were filed on the alien, and I guess we'll never know if he applied for or received deferred action.

Low Levels of Enforcement

For my testimony, I was asked to analyze a set of mostly unpublished statistics and documents on DHS enforcement activity over the last five years. This material shows that, contrary to the administration's claims that they have achieved record levels of enforcement, the number of removals is now 40 percent lower than when the Morton memo was issued in June 2011.

Removals of convicted criminals are also running 40 percent lower now than in June 2011. Removals generated by ICE's Enforcement and Removals division, which carries out most of what little interior immigration enforcement is done, are 50 percent lower now than in June 2011. This decline has occurred despite the expansion of ICE's Secure Communities program, in which ICE is notified of alien arrests in every city and county in the nation.

It's reasonable to ask: If ICE is removing so few people now than before, then how can DHS claim that they set a record for deportations last year? The answer: Because over the last several years, DHS has begun counting large numbers of Border Patrol cases in its annual removal statistics. There have always been some Border Patrol cases tallied as part of the total. But in recent years the number of Border Patrol cases has grown from about 33 percent of the total in 2008 to 56 percent so far this fiscal year. In other words, ICE's top priority now—at least as expressed in its own statistics—seems to be processing Border patrol cases, not pursuing criminal aliens in the interior, as it claims.

Even more concerning, the documents DHS provided indicate that the numbers are more than likely artificially inflated due to double-counting. Under DHS's transactional record-keeping system, each time an alien is processed by an agency, even if within a 24-hour time period, a new case file is created, and the removal counted for each part of DHS that handles the alien. Aliens who are processed under the Alien Transfer Exit Program (ATEP), which accounted for about 85,000 of the removals reported last year, were handled by Border Patrol and ICE, and potentially at least two ICE field offices could claim credit for the removal. This would mean that multiple removals were recorded for the same person.

The federal government called no witnesses to its defense.

The Obama Administration Has Weakened Interior Enforcement of Immigration Laws

Federation for American Immigration Reform

The Federation for American Immigration Reform is a nonprofit organization that seeks to improve border security, to stop illegal immigration, and to reduce immigration levels overall.

The [Barack] Obama Administration has further weakened already inadequate immigration enforcement in the interior of the country. This may be seen in four developments undertaken by agencies of the Department of Homeland Security (DHS).

- First, DHS announced that it was revising 287(g) agreements with state and local authorities to limit their scope. Those agreements, identified by the Immigration and Nationality Act section that provides for them, provide for local law enforcement personnel to be trained by the Immigration and Customs Enforcement (ICE) agency and to be deputized to act as immigration law enforcement personnel. When illegal aliens are identified by the 287(g) deputized personnel they are put into the hands of ICE for deportation. Those partnerships had become a major source of DHS deportations of more than 35,000 persons in the past two years. The revised agreements insisted on by ICE restrict the scope of the illegal aliens that ICE will accept for deportation to aliens convicted of serious felony offenses. In that

Federation for American Immigration Reform, "Department of Homeland Security's Non-Enforcement Policy," September 2010.

way, the locally trained and deputized law enforcement personnel are put in the position of having to resume a practice of "catch and release" for any other illegal aliens. Following the initiative to restrict these agreements, some of the local jurisdictions decided to leave the program rather than accept the new limitation.

- Second, the administration has virtually suspended worksite enforcement actions that apprehend illegal alien workers. It has instead substituted paper audits of the I-9 employment documents required for all new hires. This change has allowed ICE to continue to claim it is enforcing the law against employers of illegal aliens without arresting and deporting illegal workers. This practice simply identifies those employers who have not complied with the law in collecting and filing the I-9 information and those employers who have accepted fake documents. The government cannot prosecute employers for knowingly employing illegal workers unless it can be proven that the employer knew the workers presenting the fake documents were illegally in the country. This practice, billed by the Obama administration as "smart enforcement," is a radical departure from stepped-up enforcement during 2007 and 2008 when the worksite raids resulted in the apprehension of illegal workers who became a potential source of testimony regarding the hiring practices of their employers. This change in policy reduces the threat of prosecution and possible imprisonment against employers into a minor inconvenience of a monetary fine and the possible loss of services of the illegal alien employees identified as having used fake or stolen identity documents. Meanwhile, the illegal alien workers remain free to find other jobs.

- Third, ICE has developed and codified a system of triage in which it prioritizes the aliens that it seeks to apprehend and deport. There is precedent for this triage in the policies of previous administrations, and there is reason to prioritize the removal of aliens who pose a danger to society. However, the implementation of the administration's current prioritization excessively limits enforcement against virtually all other immigration violators. All police forces practice some form of discretion in deploying their manpower and resources, but it would be unheard of for them to simply abandon enforcement against all but violent criminals, who account for less than 10 percent of all crimes recorded by the FBI. The memo by ICE director, John Morton is titled "Civil Immigration Enforcement: Priorities for the Apprehension, Detention and Removal of Aliens." While national security suspects and dangerous criminal aliens should be a priority for deportation, the ICE triage system ignores the importance of removing others who have broken the immigration law and preventing crimes before they happen. Comprehensive enforcement of the immigration law will encourage attrition, i.e., the voluntary departure of illegal aliens, and deter new illegal immigration, an objective that runs contrary to the administration's political support for a sweeping amnesty.

- Fourth, under pressure from advocates for illegal aliens, who charge that the Obama administration has failed to deliver the "comprehensive immigration reform" that candidate Obama promised, the administration has explored the options for providing amnesty on a case-by-case basis to illegal aliens. The document entitled "Administrative Alternatives to Comprehensive Immigration Reform" developed by the Citizenship and Immigration Services (USCIS) branch of the Department of Homeland Security outlines measures that may be taken by discretionary administrative action. These measures, if systematically adopted would constitute a major shift in immigration enforcement policy without congressional authorization. The document states that ". . . USCIS can extend benefits and/or protections to many individuals and groups by issuing new guidance and regulations, exercising discretion with regard to parole-in-place, deferred action and the issuance of Notices to Appear (NTA), and adopting significant process improvements." Among those identified as potential beneficiaries are thousands of illegal aliens who have benefited from grants of Temporary Protected Status. The memo suggests ignoring deportable aliens who have no basis for relief from deportation while issuing NTAs for those who do have grounds for relief. Another option raised in the memo is redefining the "extreme hardship" standard for approving suspension of deportation. The memo posits, "This would encourage many more [illegally resident] spouses, sons and daughters of U.S. citizens and lawful permanent residents to seek relief without fear of removal." The administration dismissed this USCIS memo as a normal internal discussion of possibilities that has no status. The administration, tellingly, did not deny its interest in pursuing those actions. Recent well publicized cases of reprieves against deportation of illegal alien youth indicate that in all probability, the administration has already adopted a policy along the lines suggested in the planning document for illegal alien youths who would benefit if the DREAM Act [a proposed law to offer legal status to illegal immigrants brought to the United States as children] were enacted.

- Fifth, despite the administration's attempt to downplay its planning for a "stealth" amnesty by executive discre-

> tion, a further memo from ICE director Morton issued on August 20, 2010 documents that these proposed benefits for illegal aliens are already being implemented. The latest memo instructs that as many as 17,000 ICE deportation cases should be fast tracked in USCIS for dismissal of the deportation orders. All the beneficiaries need is to have a petition for relief from deportation, a petition from a U.S. citizen or legal resident family member and to not have a disqualifying criminal record. This action would not provide 'green cards' for the aliens, but it would mean they would no longer be subject to deportation and would be free to stay in the United States in the hope that a formal amnesty would eventually be adopted.

The weakening of the 287(g) program, the virtual suspension of worksite raids, the implementation of a diminished enforcement strategy through triage, and the increased refusal to deport illegal aliens are all aimed at weakening interior enforcement of the nation's immigration laws. These moves have been taken by ICE career employees as a slap in the face. The AFL-CIO affiliate National Council 118 of ICE employees issued a unanimously approved "vote of no confidence" in the director of ICE and the director of the DHS Office of Policy Planning on June 25, 2010. The union statement said, "This action reflects the growing dissatisfaction and concern among ICE employees and Union leaders that [the DHS directors] have abandoned the Agency's core mission . . . of providing for public safety, and have instead directed their attention to campaigning for programs and policies related to amnesty. . . ."

The extent to which the administration will continue to pursue this non-enforcement strategy is likely to be limited only by the extent to which there is concerted opposition to these policies in Congress and the U.S. public.

Chapter 3

Should Illegal Immigrants Be Granted a Path to Citizenship?

Chapter Preface

Today's immigration debate is reminiscent of an earlier period during the 1980s when Congress passed and President Ronald Reagan signed legislation to address the issue of millions of immigrants living in the United States without legal authorization. The law was called the Immigration Reform and Control Act (IRCA), which was passed and signed into law on November 6, 1986. At that time, the number of illegal immigrants in the country numbered only about three million, compared to approximately eleven million here currently. IRCA was designed to grant amnesty—that is, legal status and possible citizenship—to illegal immigrants already in the country while at the same time mandating stricter immigration enforcement measures to prevent future illegal immigration. The success or failure of the 1986 immigration reform effort is a major consideration for today's policy makers as they struggle to craft new immigration reform legislation.

Specifically, IRCA gave unauthorized immigrants a way to gain legal status if they met certain conditions. The main requirements applicants had to meet were (1) that they had lived and maintained a continuous physical presence in the United States since January 1, 1982; (2) that they had no criminal record; and (3) that they had registered with the US military draft system. In addition, applicants for legal status had to pay a fine, pay back taxes, and demonstrate a minimal knowledge of US history, government, and the English language (or be enrolled in an approved study program). Further, applicants were prohibited from receiving any form of public welfare assistance for five years after they gained legal status. After applicants gained permanent legal status, they could eventually apply for US citizenship.

The enforcement provisions of IRCA were designed to balance out the amnesty part by increasing border security and setting up a new system of employer sanctions to discourage the future hiring of unauthorized immigrants. For the first time, the act made it illegal for US employers to knowingly recruit or hire unauthorized immigrants and required employers to check and document their employees' identities and immigration status. This was the origin of the paper-based I-9 system, which mandated that all new job applicants fill out an Employment Eligibility Verification Form (also called an I-9 form) attesting to their identity and legal status and eligibility to work. Documents acceptable to show identity included, for example, Social Security cards, driver's licenses, and voter registration cards. Documents that were deemed acceptable to show both identity and ability to work included US passports, permanent resident cards (called green cards), or other types of unexpired temporary US visas. As long as employers acquired the proper documentation from their new hires, they could not be penalized. The law, however, provided that employers who knowingly hired illegal workers could be subjected to criminal penalties.

In the years following the enactment of IRCA, the law helped about 2.7 million unauthorized immigrants to achieve permanent legal status. Critics charge, however, that this legalization program came at a high fiscal cost to both state and federal governments. The Center for Immigration Studies, a nonpartisan research group that seeks to lower the number of immigrants to the United States, has estimated that over the first ten years after the law was passed, the IRCA program cost a total of $78.7 billion, largely in public welfare, community services, schooling, and other types of assistance to the new legal residents and their children. In addition, critics say IRCA's enforcement system was a failure. The I-9 system, many observers claim, led to the widespread use of fraudulent documents. Other critics fault the federal government for not making immigration enforcement a high priority or doing enough to tighten the US southern border. The end result was that millions more immigrants entered the United States in the decades following the passage of IRCA. By 2007, the number of illegal immigrants living in America reached a record twelve million, according to many estimates. Today, that number has shrunk slightly and most experts agree that the illegal immigrant population now numbers about eleven million.

The size of this undocumented population has reignited public discourse about immigration in the United States, especially since the US Senate has proposed, and in June 2013 passed, an immigration reform bill that closely resembles the 1986 compromise of tougher enforcement combined with amnesty. In fact, many commentators note that the current Senate bill mirrors the IRCA formula almost exactly—a legalization program (and eventual path to citizenship) for the eleven million immigrants who are in the country illegally, along with increased border enforcement and employer sanctions. Supporters of the Senate approach, however, argue that a new immigration reform law can avoid the pitfalls of IRCA. For example, technology now enables a paperless worker verification program that many people claim will eliminate the problem of fraudulent IDs. A system of electronic verification called E-Verify, in fact, has been used by many employers on a voluntary basis for a number of years, and the Senate bill mandates that this system be nationalized to cover all employers within five years. Supporters also point out that both border security and immigration enforcement has improved dramatically in recent years, and that the Senate bill further strengthens border security by authorizing more border agents and more funding for technology and fencing.

The authors of the viewpoints in this chapter of *Current Controversies: Immigration* offer a variety of opinions about what is perhaps the most controversial part of the Senate immigration reform proposal—whether today's eleven million unauthorized immigrants living in the country should be provided a path to legalization and eventual citizenship.

Granting Illegal Immigrants a Path to Citizenship Would Boost US and State Economies

Robert Lynch and Patrick Oakford

Robert Lynch is a professor of economics at Washington College in Maryland. Patrick Oakford is a research assistant at the Center for American Progress, a progressive think tank in Washington, DC.

On April 16, 2013, the Senate's "Gang of 8"—a bipartisan group of eight U.S. senators—filed the Border Security, Economic Opportunity, and Immigration Modernization Act of 2013. At the core of the bill is a provision that will provide a pathway to earned legalization and citizenship for the 11 million undocumented immigrants in America.

The pathway to citizenship for these aspiring Americans will be neither short nor easy. Under the provisions of the bill, most undocumented immigrants will have to wait 10 years before they can apply for legal permanent residency—a green card. In addition, most will not be eligible for citizenship until at least 13 years after the bill is enacted.

Despite this long process, there are significant economic benefits to the U.S. economy and to all Americans when unauthorized immigrants acquire provisional legal status. Our prior research in a Center for American Progress report, "Economic Effects of Granting Legal Status and Citizenship to Undocumented Immigrants," showed that legalization and citizenship bring large economic benefits to the nation as a whole. But as this brief will show, the economies of each state also stand to gain large benefits if immigrants are put on a path to

Robert Lynch and Patrick Oakford, "National and State-by-State Economic Benefits of Immigration Reform," *Center for American Progress*, May 17, 2013.

legal status and citizenship. In this follow-up issue brief, we break down the economic gains for 24 individual states.

Both the acquisition of legal status and citizenship enable undocumented immigrants to produce and earn significantly more. These resulting productivity and wage gains ripple through the economy because immigrants are not just workers—they are also taxpayers and consumers. They pay taxes on their higher wages and they spend their increased earnings on the purchase of goods and services including food, clothing, and homes. This increased consumption boosts business sales, expands the economy, generates new jobs, and increases the earnings of all Americans.

Each state will experience significant economic growth as well. In this follow-up to the "Economic Effects of Granting Legal Status and Citizenship to Undocumented Immigrants," we begin by recapping the national gains. We then provide estimates of the economic benefits for 24 states if their undocumented populations were legalized. Specifically, we estimate the increases over 10 years in gross state product, or GSP [a measure of a state's total economic output], as well as earnings, taxes, and jobs for these states if the Senate Gang of 8's bill is enacted in 2013. We also explain why immigration reform is responsible for these specific economic benefits. The methodology for this brief relies upon estimates of the undocumented population in each state and replicates the methodology used in our previous report.

National Economic Benefits of Legalization and a Pathway to Citizenship

If the 11.1 million undocumented immigrants currently living in the United States were provided legal status, then the 10-year cumulative increase in the gross domestic product, or GDP [a measure of total economic output], of the United States would be $832 billion. Similarly, the cumulative increase in the personal income of all Americans over 10 years would be $470 billion. On average over 10 years, immigration reform would create 121,000 new jobs each year. Undocumented immigrants would also benefit and contribute more to the U.S. economy. Over the 10-year period they would earn $392 billion more and pay an additional $109 billion in taxes—$69 billion to the federal government and $40 billion to state and local governments. After 10 years, when the undocumented immigrants start earning citizenship, they will experience additional increases in their income on the order of 10 percent, which will in turn further boost our economy.

State-by-State Economic Benefits of Legalization and a Pathway to Citizenship

The economic benefits of legalization have been calculated for 24 states where 88 percent of the 11 million undocumented immigrants reside. Across all of these states, the economic gains are significant. In Arizona, for example, the 10-year cumulative increase in GSP will be $23.1 billion, the increase in the earnings of state residents will be $15.3 billion, and immigration reform will create an average of an additional 3,400 jobs annually. In addition to these significant gains, undocumented immigrants themselves will experience significant increases in their income and pay more taxes to their states. In Arizona, for example, over the 10-year period they will earn $12.7 billion more and pay an additional $1.5 billion in state and local taxes on these increased earnings.

Legalization and citizenship facilitate the labor-market mobility of the undocumented, which boosts wages and improves economic efficiency.

In each of these states, when the undocumented immigrants eventually gain citizenship, their earnings will increase an additional 10 percent, further improving the economy and prosperity of all residents in their state. But since the attainment of citizenship will occur outside of the 10-year window of analysis of this study, we do not include any of the economic benefits from the acquisition of citizenship. In addition, we do not include the $69 billion in additional federal taxes that the undocumented would pay on their increased earnings. . . .

Why Legalization and Citizenship Improve Economic Outcomes and Boost the Earnings of Undocumented Immigrants

There are many reasons why receiving legal status and citizenship raises the incomes of immigrants and improves economic outcomes. Five main reasons are explained below.

Investment in Education and Training

Legalization and citizenship promote investment in the education and training of immigrants that eventually pays off in the form of higher wages and output. Legal status and citizenship provide a guarantee of long-term membership in American society and cause noncitizen immigrants to invest heavily in their English language skills and in other forms of education and training that raise their productivity and earnings.

Labor Mobility and Efficiency

Legalization and citizenship facilitate the labor-market mobility of the undocumented, which boosts wages and improves economic efficiency. Prior to legalization, unauthorized immigrants are subject to deportation if apprehended and, regardless of their skills, tend to pursue employment in low-paying, low-profile occupations—such as farming, child care, or cleaning services—where their legal status is less likely to be discovered. Thus, undocumented workers do not receive the same market returns on their skills that comparable but legal workers receive. In other words, the productivity of the legalized improves in part because workers move to sectors where their skills and education are both valued and relevant to the work being conducted. Therefore, legalization and citizenship improve the efficiency of the labor market by ensuring that people are working in fields where their skillsets and training are being used to the fullest extent.

Legal Protections

Providing legal status and citizenship to undocumented immigrants gives them legal protections that raise their wages. Legalization allows the newly authorized to invoke employment rights and increases their bargaining power relative to their employers. This means that newly legal immigrants are better equipped to contest an unlawful termination of employment, to negotiate for fair compensation or a promotion, and to file a complaint if they are being mistreated or abused.

Access to Better Jobs

Legal status and citizenship provide access to a broader range of higher-paying jobs. Many jobs, including many public-sector and high-paying private-sector jobs, are available only to legal residents or citizens. In addition, employers often prefer to hire citizens over noncitizens.

Fostering Entrepreneurship

Legal status and citizenship make it easier for immigrants to start businesses and create jobs. These facilitate entrepreneurship by providing access to licenses, permits, insurance, and credit—all of which make it easier to start businesses and create jobs. Despite the legal obstacles to entrepreneurship that noncitizens currently face, immigrants are more likely to own a business and start a new business than are native-born Americans. Thus, immigration reform that unleashes this creative potential of immigrant entrepreneurs promotes economic growth, higher incomes, and more job opportunities. . . .

A Win for Immigrants and Americans

Undocumented immigrants are currently earning far less than their potential and therefore paying much less in taxes than they otherwise would be. Overall, they are contributing significantly less to the U.S. economy than they potentially could. With legalization and citizenship, undocumented immigrants will produce and earn more, pay more in taxes, boost the American economy, increase the incomes of all Americans, and promote job growth. This analysis of the economic impact on 24 states, many with the largest undocumented populations, demonstrates that it is not just the nation but also each individual state that will benefit from immigration reform. The sooner we grant legal status and provide a pathway to citizenship to undocumented immigrants, the sooner all Americans will be able to reap these benefits.

There Are Many Reasons to Grant Amnesty to Illegal Immigrants

Ed Krayewski

Ed Krayewski is an associate editor for Reason, *a monthly magazine and website that espouses a libertarian point of view that embraces liberty and individual choice.*

Immigration reform returned to center stage in Washington last week with a proposal from a bipartisan group of senators that was promptly endorsed in principle by President Barack Obama. One of the lynchpins of the proposal is providing a "path to citizenship" for those who are currently in the country illegally, a concept that opponents were quick to label "amnesty." Obama of course denies any talk of amnesty, saying instead that he wants illegal immigrants to pay penalties, pay taxes, learn English, and then go "to the back of the line."

But what's wrong with granting amnesty to hard-working, tax-paying individuals whose only crime is their immigration status? Indeed, amnesty is not only the best solution to our immigration problem, it is the *only* feasible solution. Here are five reasons to grant amnesty to illegal immigrants now.

Immigration Is Good for the Economy

For all the rhetoric about immigrants stealing jobs, immigration actually provides a benefit to the national economy, whether those immigrants crossed the border legally or not. Why? Because of what economists call the specialization of labor. As Jonathan Hoenig, proprietor of the Capitalist Pig blog, explains: "The fact that foreigners are eager to pick crops, clean houses, bus tables and produce allows more of us to afford cheaper food and better services, affording us even more wealth to enjoy and invest. It's not the immigrants, but the taxes, spending and entitlements (most of which immigrants don't even receive) that have drained the economy dry."

Illegal Immigrants Already Pay Taxes

One of President Obama's markers on the path to citizenship is "paying taxes," but most illegal immigrants already do so. As Reason Foundation Senior Analyst Shikha Dalmia has reported, in 2006 an estimated 8 million illegal immigrants—up to two thirds of the total—paid taxes, including both income taxes and Medicare and Social Security taxes. Indeed, revenue from illegal immigrants is estimated at $11 billion a year to Social Security alone, and there's not even a pretense of those payments leading to eventual benefits. And of course everyone who buys things in the U.S. pays sales taxes, irrespective of their immigration status. Undoubtedly, even more illegal immigrants would pay taxes if they didn't have to worry about possible deportation as a consequence.

> *It would be exceedingly difficult to deport [all illegal immigrants]—if not totally impossible. Indeed, even attempting to do so would require a massive expansion of government bureaucracy.*

Most Illegal Immigrants Are Otherwise Law-Abiding

While illegal immigration is a crime, the act of crossing the border without authorization is a mere misdemeanor. Immigrants, in fact, may help drive crime down. The vast majority want to stay in the country in order to work and so naturally steer clear of breaking any laws. And as The Future of Freedom Foundation's Sheldon Richman pointed out a few years ago, all manners of violent crimes dropped dramatically since 1986, the last time an amnesty was granted to illegal immigrants. Yes, 14 percent of federal inmates are illegal immigrants, but they are largely there for immigration violations. On the state level, Richman notes, less than 5 percent of inmates are illegal immigrants. Not exactly the makings of a crime wave.

Immigration Is a Natural Right

Last week, Judge Andrew Napolitano explained here at Reason.com that immigration is a natural right. What does that mean? A natural right is a right inherent to our humanity, and the freedom of movement is such a right. The idea that immigration needs to be "authorized" by the government flies in the face of that freedom. Immigrants who come to America seeking the opportunity to work and pursue happiness, or those brought here at too young an age to have any say in the matter, ought to be able to stay to pursue those opportunities. Conversely, employers ought to be able to enter into contracts with any would-be employees they please. The government doesn't own the country and political borders are just lines on maps. Treating law-abiding people like criminals simply because they didn't meet the bureaucratic requirements of migration abrogates their natural right to travel and Americans' natural right to freely associate and make contracts.

There Are Too Many Illegal Immigrants to Do Anything Else

According to the latest estimates, there are about 11 million illegal immigrants in America. That's a lot of people. It would be exceedingly difficult to deport them all—if not totally impossible. Indeed, even attempting to do so would require a massive expansion of government bureaucracy, particularly in the form of new government workers to round up illegal immigrants, process them, and deport them. The inhumanity of this approach goes without saying: Individuals would be ripped away from their families and communities. And there would also be dire economic consequences from removing millions of hard-working residents from the domestic labor pool.

It's time to face the facts: The millions of illegal immigrants currently residing in the United States are overwhelmingly law-abiding, tax-paying, and hard-working. Grant them amnesty and let them continue to make America a better place.

Most Americans Support Allowing Illegal Immigrants to Stay in the United States

Pew Center for People and the Press

The Pew Center for People and the Press is a research project of the Pew Research Center, a nonpartisan "fact tank" that informs the public about the issues, attitudes, and trends shaping America and the world.

A new survey finds that seven-in-ten Americans (71%) say there should be a way for people in the United States illegally to remain in this country if they meet certain requirements, while 27% say they should not be allowed to stay legally. Most who favor providing illegal immigrants with some form of legal status—43% of the public—say they should be allowed to apply for citizenship, but 24% of the public says they should only be allowed to apply for legal residency.

Majorities across all demographic and political groups say there should be a way for illegal immigrants who meet certain requirements to stay in the U.S. legally. Among those who favor providing legal status, the balance of opinion is in favor of allowing those here illegally who meet the requirements to apply for citizenship. However, no more than about half in any demographic group supports permitting illegal immigrants to apply for citizenship.

In 2011, there were about 40 million immigrants in the United States. Of that total, 11.1 million, or 28%, were in this country illegally.

The national survey by the Pew Research Center, conducted March 13–17 [2013] among 1,501 adults, finds that

Pew Center for People and the Press, "Most Say Illegal Immigrants Should Be Allowed to Stay, But Citizenship Is More Divisive," March 28, 2013.

overall attitudes about immigrants in the United States are more positive than negative, despite the nation's struggling economy.

Thinking about immigrants generally, 49% of Americans say they strengthen the country because of their hard work and talents, while 41% say they are a burden because they take jobs, health care and housing. In a June 2010 poll, 39% said immigrants strengthened the country while 50% said they were a burden.

In addition, more Americans think that the growing number of newcomers in the United States strengthens society than believe that they threaten traditional American customs and values. About half (52%) say the growing number of newcomers in the U.S. strengthens society, while 43% say the influx of newcomers threatens traditional American values and customs.

Currently, 49% agree with the statement "immigrants today strengthen the country because of their hard work and talents."

Broad Support for Legal Status for Illegal Immigrants

Support for granting legal status to illegal immigrants is wide ranging. Eight-in-ten non-Hispanic blacks (82%) and Hispanics (80%) say those in the United States illegally should be allowed to stay if they meet certain requirements; about half of blacks (52%) and Hispanics (49%) say illegal immigrants should be able to apply for citizenship.

Two-thirds of non-Hispanic whites (67%) say illegal immigrants should be allowed to stay in the country legally, while 31% say they should not. Four-in-ten whites say people in the United States illegally should have the chance to apply for citizenship if they meet certain requirements.

Among whites with no college degree, 61% favor allowing those in the U.S. illegally to stay legally, while 37% disagree. There is more support among white college graduates for permitting illegal immigrants to stay in the country legally (81% say they should, while just 17% say they should not).

The partisan differences over providing some form of legal status for illegal immigrants are modest: 76% of Democrats, 70% of independents and 64% of Republicans say illegal immigrants should be allowed to stay in the United States if they meet certain requirements.

Whites in both parties are divided along educational lines over how to deal with illegal immigrants in the United States: Among white Democrats and Democratic-leaning independents, 92% of college graduates favor allowing illegal immigrants to stay in the U.S. legally if they meet certain requirements; support falls to 68% among white Democrats and Democratic leaners who have not completed college. Similarly, there is a 20-point education gap among white Republicans and GOP-leaning independents (75% of college graduates vs. 55% of non-college grads).

Opinions About Immigrants' Impact on the Country

Currently, 49% agree with the statement "immigrants today strengthen the country because of their hard work and talents." Somewhat fewer (41%) agree with an opposing statement: "immigrants today are a burden on our country because they take our jobs, housing and health care."

The balance of opinion on these questions has fluctuated over the years. Two years ago, opinions were evenly divided and in June 2010, more said that immigrants were a burden than a strength for the United States (50% vs. 39%).

Nearly two decades ago, in July 1994, 63% viewed immigrants as a burden, but the percentage expressing this view declined substantially by the end of the 1990s (to 38% in September 2000).

In recent years, there has been little change in opinions about the impact of newcomers from other countries on traditional values. About half (52%) say the growing number of newcomers to the United States strengthens American society, while 43% say they threaten traditional American customs and values.

Racial, Ethnic, Partisan Differences in Views of Immigrants

While majorities across all groups support legal status for illegal immigrants, there are sharp differences in opinions about the impact of immigrants on the country. Opinions about immigrants have become somewhat more positive among most groups since 2010.

College graduates express far more positive opinions about the impact of immigrants than do those with less education.

Fully 74% of Hispanics say that immigrants strengthen the country because of their hard work and talents. About half of blacks (52%) also say that immigrants strengthen the country, compared with just 41% of whites.

While most Democrats (58%) say that immigrants strengthen the country because of their hard work and talents, most Republicans (55%) say they are a burden because they take jobs and health care.

College graduates express far more positive opinions about the impact of immigrants than do those with less education. Fully 67% say immigrants strengthen the country, compared with 41% of those with no more than a high school education.

By a wide margin (59% to 33%), more 18-to-29 year-olds say that immigrants strengthen the country than say they are burden. Among those 65 and older, more say immigrants are a burden (49%) than a strength (37%).

Opinions about whether the growing number of newcomers to the United States strengthens society or threatens American values break down along similar lines. Whites are divided (45% vs. 49%). Majorities of Hispanics (67%) and blacks (62%) say the growing number of newcomers strengthens American society.

Majorities of Democrats (61%) and independents (55%) say that the increasing number of newcomers strengthens society; just 34% of Republicans agree.

Religion and Views of Immigrants

Majorities of all major religious groups say there should be a way for immigrants who are currently in the U.S. illegally and who meet certain requirements to stay in the country.

For the most part, those who favor legal status for illegal immigrants say they should be allowed to apply for citizenship.

Opinions among major religious groups are more divided when it comes to the impact of immigrants on the country.

A majority of white evangelical Protestants (55%) say that immigrants are a burden because they take jobs, housing and health care, while about as many (58%) say they threaten traditional American customs and values.

Other religious groups have less negative views of the impact of immigrants. These differences in opinions, however, are largely the result of underlying differences between religious groups in race, political ideology, party identification and other factors; after controlling for these factors, the independent impact of religion is minimal.

A Path to Citizenship for Illegal Immigrants Would Cost US Taxpayers Trillions

Carrie Dann

Carrie Dann is a political reporter for First Read, *an NBC News blog.*

A new study from the conservative Heritage Foundation [think tank] estimates that granting a path to citizenship for illegal immigrants will cost US taxpayers at least $6.3 trillion.

Heritage Foundation scholar Robert Rector co-authored the long-anticipated study, which is sure to be cited frequently by foes of the immigration reform effort as lawmakers take up legislation to overhaul the nation's system.

But the study also drew swift criticism from Republicans supporting the reform effort, who called the Heritage Foundation's estimate politicized, exaggerated and flawed in its methodology.

The $6.3 Trillion Calculation

The $6.3 trillion calculation derives from the federal benefits Rector and co-author Jason Richwine believe an estimated 11 million newly legalized immigrants will receive over their lifetimes versus the taxes they will pay.

A summary of the report, for example, states that "former unlawful immigrants together would receive $9.4 trillion in government benefits and services and pay $3.1 trillion in taxes, for a lifetime 'fiscal deficit'—at minimum—of $6.3 trillion (total benefits minus total taxes.)"

Carrie Dann, "Conservative Group Pegs Cost of 'Path to Citizenship' at $6.3T," NBC news.com, May 6, 2013.

Those benefits, the study states, will eventually include means-tested welfare benefits and health care as well as Social Security payments.

The report's authors acknowledge that their estimated price tag concentrates only on the citizenship piece of proposed immigration reform legislation rather than estimating the costs of the massive bill as a whole. But they argue that the economic benefits of a comprehensive reform that includes a path to citizenship would still be minimal compared to cost of "amnesty."

"No sensible thinking person could read this study and conclude that over 50 years that this could possibly have a positive economic impact," said Heritage president and former senator Jim DeMint at a press conference unveiling the study.

The Cumulative Effect of Immigration Reform

Under the Gang of Eight proposal [a reference to eight US senators who cosponsored an immigration reform bill] that was introduced in the Senate last month [April 2013], qualified undocumented workers could pay fines and back taxes to become eligible to apply for a probationary legal status that—after 10 years, more fines and a clean criminal record—can be adjusted to legal permanent residency and ultimately citizenship.

During that probationary status, previously undocumented immigrants would not be eligible to receive federal benefits like welfare.

But Rector states that, because the average age of an undocumented immigrant is just 34 years old, the accumulated benefits after these individuals become citizens will far outweigh their contributions to the economy.

That's a calculation that others in conservative community dismiss, including economists like Doug Holtz-Eakin and policy analysts at the [libertarian] Cato Institute who dispute the Heritage Foundation's methodology and say that the estimate fails to take into account the cumulative effects of immigration reform on America's economy.

In a conference call sponsored by the Bipartisan Policy Center, former Mississippi governor and onetime RNC [Republican National Committee] head Haley Barbour slammed Heritage's report as a "political document" designed to scare off Republicans inclined to support comprehensive reform.

"That Heritage is trying to kill this in the crib now, I think, is a political statement that they know that this is going to be a movement for reform that's going to get stronger and stronger because it's truly good policy," he said.

And Sen. Jeff Flake, a Republican member of the Senate's Gang of Eight, took to Twitter to blast the study shortly after its release.

"Here we go again," he wrote. "New Heritage study claims huge cost for Immigration Reform. Ignores economic benefits. No dynamic scoring."

The DREAM Act Would Cost Taxpayers Billions of Dollars

Steven A. Camarota

Steven A. Camarota is the director of research at the Center for Immigration Studies, a nonpartisan, nonprofit, research organization that provides policy makers and others with information about the social and economic consequences of legal and illegal immigration into the United States.

This *Memorandum* examines the costs and likely impact of the DREAM Act currently [2010] being considered by Congress. The act offers permanent legal status to illegal immigrants up to age 35 who arrived in the United States before age 16 provided they complete two years of college. Under the act, beneficiaries would receive in-state tuition. Given the low income of illegal immigrants, most can be expected to attend state schools, with a cost to taxpayers in the billions of dollars. As both funds and slots are limited at state universities and community colleges, the act may reduce the educational opportunities available to U.S. citizens.

The Impact of the DREAM Act

Among the findings:

- Assuming no fraud, we conservatively estimate that 1.03 million illegal immigrants will eventually enroll in public institutions (state universities or community colleges) as a result of the DREAM Act. That is, they meet the residence and age requirements of the act, have graduated high school, or will do so, and will come forward.

Steven A. Camarota, "Estimating the Impact of the DREAM Act," *Center for Immigration Studies*, November 2010.

- On average, each illegal immigrant who attends a public institution will receive a tuition subsidy from taxpayers of nearly $6,000 for each year he or she attends, for total cost of $6.2 billion a year, not including other forms of financial assistance they may also receive.
- The above estimate is for the number who will enroll in public institutions. A large share of those who attend college may not complete the two full years necessary to receive permanent residence.
- The cost estimate assumes that the overwhelming majority will enroll in community colleges, which are much cheaper for students and taxpayers than state universities.
- The estimate is only for new students not yet enrolled. It does not include illegal immigrants currently enrolled at public institutions or those who have already completed two years of college. Moreover, it does not include the modest number of illegal immigrants who are expected to attend private institutions.
- The DREAM Act does not provide funding to states and counties to cover the costs it imposes. Since enrollment and funding are limited at public institutions, the act's passage will require some combination of tuition increases, tax increases to expand enrollment, or a reduction in spaces available for American citizens at these schools.
- Tuition hikes will be particularly difficult for students, as many Americans already find it difficult to pay for college. Research indicates that one out of three college students drops out before receiving a degree. Costs are a major reason for the high dropout rate.
- In 2009 there were 10.2 million U.S. citizens under age 35 who had dropped out of college without receiving a

degree. There were an additional 15.2 million citizens under age 35 who had completed high school, but never attended college.

- Lawmakers need to consider the strains the DREAM Act will create and the impact of adding roughly one million students to state universities and community colleges on the educational opportunities available to American citizens.
- Providing state schools with added financial support to offset the costs of the DREAM Act would avoid the fiscal costs at the state and local level, but it would shift the costs to federal taxpayers.
- Advocates of the DREAM Act argue that it will significantly increase tax revenue, because with a college education, recipients will earn more and pay more in taxes over their lifetime. However, several factors need to be considered when evaluating this argument:
    - Any hoped-for tax benefit is in the long-term, and will not help public institutions deal with the large influx of new students the act creates in the short-term.
    - Given limited spaces at public institutions, there will almost certainly be some crowding out of U.S. citizens—reducing their lifetime earnings and tax payments.
    - The DREAM Act only requires two years of college; no degree is necessary. The income gains for having some college, but no degree, are modest.
    - Because college dropout rates are high, many illegal immigrants who enroll at public institutions will not complete the two years the act requires, so taxpayers will bear the expense without a long-term benefit.

Data and Methods

When estimating the immediate costs of the DREAM Act, there are two key methodological issues that have to be resolved. First, how many illegal immigrants are potentially eligible. Second, how many would come forward and enroll in college, particularly at state schools? The size of the illegal immigrant population, the share who would come forward for amnesty, and the potential for fraudulent applications all make for a degree of uncertainty when estimating the number of beneficiaries and the costs associated with the DREAM Act.

We think it likely that 95 percent . . . of the 1.266 million illegal immigrants who could qualify will eventually come forward to register for provisional legal status under the DREAM Act.

Number of Potential Beneficiaries. Based on an analysis of the 2006 to 2008 public-use files of the Current Population Survey (CPS), the Migration Policy Institute (MPI), working with Jeffrey S. Passel of the Pew Hispanic Center, has estimated a total of 2.15 million persons who might qualify for the DREAM Act. Our analysis of the 2009 and 2010 CPS indicates that the number of potentially eligible illegal immigrants has declined by 7 percent, for a total of 1.998 million illegal immigrants who meet the age and residency requirements. For the most part, in the estimates below we rely on MPI's population share, but put in our slightly updated numbers for 2009 and 2010.

We think MPI's estimate is correct that, of those who meet the age and residency requirement, 43 percent (859,000) are under age 18 and 57 percent (1.139 million) are adults. Of the 1.139 million adults who could potentially benefit from the DREAM act, 5 percent (100,000) have already completed two years of college. Of the remaining 1.039 million adults, we estimate that 51 percent (530,000) have graduated high school.

MPI estimates that 56 percent of these adults have completed high school. This difference slightly reduces our estimate for the number of potential beneficiaries of the DREAM Act compared to MPI's estimate.

In addition to the 530,000 adult high school graduates who could benefit from the act, we estimate there are 509,000 adults who have not graduated high school, but meet the act's age and residency requirements. MPI's work is not entirely clear on what share of these high school dropouts expect to eventually receive GEDs, but what is provided in their report suggests that 13 percent of these individuals will eventually get a GED. This is a reasonable estimate and, if correct, it would mean that 66,000 adult drop-outs will eventually complete high school and could enroll in college. MPI also estimates that 85 percent (730,000) of the children (currently under age 18) who meet the residency and age requirements of the DREAM Act will eventually graduate high school. Since we are interested in the added future costs of the act, we need to subtract from the above estimates the 60,000 illegal immigrants already enrolled in college at state expense. Thus, the total potential population of those who might enroll in college, but who are not enrolled and have not completed two years of college is 1.266 million (530,000 + 66,000 + 730,000 − 60,000). Again these figures do not include the roughly 100,000 illegal immigrants who have already completed two or more years of college and meet the act's age and residency requirements.

Number Who Will Enroll in College. There is no way to know for certain what fraction of illegal immigrants who meet or will meet the DREAM Act's age and residency will come forward and enroll in college. In the 1986 IRCA amnesty only a small share of potential amnesty beneficiaries did not come forward. Given that the illegal immigrants who can benefit from the DREAM Act have grown up in the United States in most cases, and the act allows six years to complete its requirements, we think it likely that 95 percent (1.203 million) of the 1.266 million illegal immigrants who could qualify will eventually come forward to register for provisional legal status under the DREAM Act. Of the 1.203 million high school graduates who will come forward, we assume 50,000 will enroll in the military, which leaves 1.154 million potential new college students. Our estimate for the military is consistent with MPI's estimate. We estimate that 90 percent (1.038 million) of the 1.154 million high school graduates will enroll in public institutions (state universities and community colleges). The remaining 10 percent will enroll in private universities. Of those that enroll in public institutions, we assume that 80 percent will attend community colleges and 20 percent will enroll in state universities.

Impact on Taxpayers. To estimate the cost to taxpayers of 1.038 million new students at public institutions of higher learning, we use the 10 states with the largest illegal immigrant populations as reported by the Department of Homeland Security.... It is true that all students who attend college, even those that pay out-of-state tuition, receive indirect subsidies from taxpayers, but for the purposes of this analysis we ignore these added costs. If these costs were added into the estimate it would increase the fiscal burden created by the DREAM Act. To estimate the average costs illegal immigrants will create at community colleges we use the county or counties where illegal immigrants are concentrated in these 10 states.

The DREAM Act does not provide funding to states and counties to cover the costs it imposes.

Given the state distribution of illegal immigrants, and assuming an 80 percent/20 percent split between community colleges and state universities, the average per-year cost for the enrolled illegal immigrants students would be $5,970. This individual cost combined with our estimate of 1.038 million new students enrolled at public institutions of higher learning would create a total cost of $6.2 billion a year for each year these students are enrolled, assuming the current fee structure. In light of the age and educational distribution of those eligible for the DREAM Act discussed earlier, about half a million new students can be expected to enroll in public institutions soon after the act is passed, with the remaining half million coming enrolling over the next decade and half.

Our estimate can be seen as conservative because it only includes taxpayer-provided tuition subsidies to in-state students, not the costs of providing student loans, work study, or any other taxpayer-provided assistance that college students often receive. There is confusion over what financial aid DREAM Act beneficiaries will be eligible to receive. Both the current House and Senate versions of the bill allow recipients to get student loans, which are directly subsidized by taxpayers. In the Senate version of the bill, illegal immigrants cannot receive PELL grants, while the House version of the act, as currently written, would seem to allow some illegal immigrants to receive PELL grants. It should also be remembered that a significant share of these new students will likely drop out. The academic preparation of many of these students is limited as are their financial resources. These factors will work against high rates of completing two years of college.

Impact on American Students. Much of the discussion of the DREAM Act has focused on the potential benefit it will create for those that receive the amnesty. Almost no attention has been paid to the impact on American citizens. The DREAM Act does not provide funding to states and counties to cover the costs it imposes. The $6.2 billion estimated cost reported above will have to be absorbed by state and local governments already struggling to close massive budget shortfalls. Public institutions of higher education, especially community colleges, have been hard hit by the drop in tax revenue caused by the current recession. Many are struggling to meet the current demand for enrollment. Since enrollment and funding are limited at public institutions, the act's passage will require some combination of tuition increases, tax increases to expand enrollment, or a reduction in spaces available for American citizens at these schools.

Tuition hikes will be particularly hard on students, as many Americans already find it difficult to pay for college. Some research indicates that one in three American college students drops out before receiving a degree. Costs are a major reason for the high dropout rate. In 2009, there were 10.2 million U.S. citizens under age 35 who had dropped out of college without receiving a degree. More than one in three of these college dropouts live in or near poverty. There were another 15.2 million citizens under age 35 who had completed high school, but never attended college. Nearly half of these younger citizens with no college experience live in or near poverty.

There is clearly a huge population of citizens who can or do attend college. Lawmakers need to consider the strains the DREAM Act will create and the impact of adding one million students to state universities and community colleges on the educational opportunities available to American Citizens.

Negative Impacts for Americans

Supporters of the DREAM Act have emphasized the often-compelling stories of illegal immigrants brought to the United States as children. But there has been almost no discussion of the likely impact the act would have on public institutions of higher learning and the American citizens and legal immigrants who wish to attend these same institutions. Given the income of most illegal immigrant families, the overwhelming majority can be expected to attend community colleges and state universities, which are much cheaper than private institutions.

Enrollment and funding at American's public institutions of higher learning are limited. As a result, passage of the DREAM Act will likely have significant negative implications for American citizens who wish to attend these same schools. Many of these institutions are already under enormous fiscal strain, as state and local governments struggle to close large budgetary shortfalls. The DREAM Act does not provide funding to states and counties to cover the costs it imposes. To deal with the added enrollment the act will create, public institutions will have to increase tuition, increase taxes, or reduce the number of spaces available for American citizens at these schools. Many Americans already find it difficult to pay for college. Research indicates that at least one in three American college students drops out before receiving a degree.

[The] passage of the DREAM act is likely to reduce the lifetime earnings of U.S. citizens who might have attended or otherwise completed college, but who are crowded or priced out of such opportunities by the DREAM Act.

Advocates of the DREAM act argue that it will significantly increase tax revenue because the DREAM Act recipients will earn much more money over the course of their lifetimes. It is certainly true that college graduates earn dramatically more than those with only a high school diploma. But even if the lifetime income and tax payments of DREAM Act recipients is enhanced in the manner supporters hope, those benefits are all in the long-term and provide no assistance to public institution dealing with the influx the act creates in the short-term.

In addition, the difference in earnings between high school graduates and those with some college but no degree is not so great. The DREAM Act requires only that two years of college be completed; no degree, not even an associate's, is necessary to gain permanent legal status. In 2009, foreign-born Hispanic high school graduates earned 77 percent as much as someone who had attended college, but not received a degree. Perhaps most importantly, any argument that the act will increase tax revenue in the long-run has to address the fact that adding this many new students to public institutions of higher learning will have some negative impact on the college enrollment of U.S. citizens given the limited funds and spaces available at public initiations. Thus, passage of the DREAM act is likely to reduce the lifetime earnings of U.S. citizens who might have attended or otherwise completed college, but who are crowded or priced out of such opportunities by the DREAM Act.

We know that the college drop-out rate is very high. There are more than 10 million U.S. citizen college drop-outs under age 35 in the United States. One way to deal with the burden the DREAM Act creates is for it to include funding that would offset the costs the act creates for state and local governments. In its current form, the act provides no such funding. We have estimated that, given the number of eligible recipients and their distribution across states, the likely costs to tax payers would be $6.2 billion a year. This estimate provides a good starting point for the size of the funding Washington would need to provide public institutions of higher learning to avoid reducing educational opportunities for U.S. citizens and legal immigrants.

CHAPTER 4

Will Proposed Immigration Reform Improve the US Immigration System?

Chapter Overview

Brianna Lee

Brianna Lee is a senior production editor for the Council on Foreign Relations, an independent membership organization, think tank, and publisher.

U.S. immigration policy has been a touchstone for political debate for decades, as policymakers weigh the need to maintain global competitiveness by attracting top foreign talent against the need to curb illegal immigration and secure U.S. borders. Most recently, the debate has focused on how to streamline a heavily bureaucratic visa application process and address the millions of undocumented immigrants already in the United States—particularly young people brought here by their parents—as well as implementing policy at the local level without jeopardizing public trust within immigrant communities.

Federal legislation on comprehensive reform has stalled in recent years, and the [Barack] Obama administration leaned toward enforcement-based policies for curbing illegal immigration during his first term. Meanwhile, restrictive state-level immigration laws—including Arizona's controversial SB 1070—have highlighted the blurry divide between state and federal authority over immigration policy. However, following President Obama's reelection in 2012, the administration and Congressional lawmakers have signaled a new willingness to make a bipartisan effort to tackle comprehensive immigration reform.

Status of the Current Immigration Debate

Public discourse is divided over the issue of illegal immigration. Opponents argue that undocumented immigrants are an economic drain; others say they are an economic boon. Some

Brianna Lee, "The US Immigration Debate," Council on Foreign Relations, April 19, 2013. Reproduced by permission.

contend that undocumented workers take jobs that would otherwise be held by American workers, while others argue they do work that Americans are unwilling to undertake. Meanwhile, many experts say that legal immigration must be made more efficient to deter illegal immigration and attract skilled foreign workers, but that the debate over illegal immigration enforcement has blocked progress on broader reform.

The federal government has employed an enforcement-heavy approach to immigration control under President Obama.

Many Americans think the U.S. immigration system is urgently in need of reform. A January 2013 Gallup poll found that only 36 percent of Americans are satisfied with the current level of immigration into the United States.

Debates center primarily on immigrants entering from Mexico—although studies by the Pew Hispanic Center show that migration flows between Mexico and the United States have been at net zero since 2007, primarily due to declining U.S. economic opportunity. This new trend "does fundamentally change the nature of U.S.-bound immigration, likely permanently," writes CFR's [Council on Foreign Relations] Shannon O'Neil, noting that the shift "has yet to feed into U.S. political debates."

An Enforcement-Based Approach to Illegal Immigration

The federal government has employed an enforcement-heavy approach to immigration control under President Obama. More than 20,000 U.S. Border Patrol agents operate along the borders—the highest number deployed in U.S. history and twice the level of a decade ago. The Obama administration has also conducted a series of nationwide immigration sweeps to arrest undocumented criminal offenders and increased audits of companies hiring unauthorized workers. President Obama's policies have also resulted in record-high deportation levels, with nearly 400,000 undocumented immigrants deported in 2011, compared to 281,000 deportations just five years prior.

The administration has also expanded the Secure Communities program, started in 2008, which allows local law enforcement to share fingerprints of arrestees with the Immigration Customs and Enforcement (ICE) agency to examine their status and criminal history for possible deportation. Secure Communities has provoked harsh criticism in some states, where critics say it has led to deportations for minor offenses rather than being applied only to "the most dangerous and violent offenders" as intended, eroding trust between immigrant communities and law enforcement. This criticism, as well as a heavily backlogged immigration court system, has led ICE to refine its deportation priorities and procedures to target high-level offenders.

The federal government's policies are criticized by immigration advocates and hardliners alike. Many conservatives argue that the administration is not doing enough to curb illegal immigration, and that allowing thousands of lower-level offenders to remain in the country amounts to "backdoor amnesty." To further deter illegal immigration, several politicians have supported the idea of an expanded fence along the U.S.-Mexico border.

In contrast, immigrant rights advocates argue that an enforcement-heavy approach instills a culture of fear in immigrant communities, and that such policies are out of touch with the reality of migration trends. Many analysts support comprehensive immigration reform that emphasizes streamlining legal pathways to citizenship in addition to enforcement policies.

CFR's Edward Alden says the White House's enforcement-based approach to illegal immigration represents a "Catch-22 situation." Overall deportation numbers will eventually drop as a result of expelling those who fall under high-priority categories, he says. Thus, the administration would become vulnerable to accusations of being "soft on enforcement."

Reforming Legal Immigration

Reforming the cumbersome visa and citizenship process for immigrants—particularly skilled foreign workers in high-demand STEM (science, technology, engineering, and math) fields—is a priority to ensure that the country retains its competitiveness in the global economy, say some experts and politicians, who are concerned about the prospect of a "reverse brain drain."

The DREAM Act would provide a pathway to citizenship for undocumented youth who immigrated as children with their families to the United States.

The U.S. visa system has long been hobbled by prolonged waiting periods, at times lasting years, resulting in part from rigid quotas. Currently, the United States issues 140,000 green cards a year for employment-based immigrants, of which no more than 7 percent can go to applicants from any one country. Applicants from India and China tend to greatly outnumber those from other countries, and therefore face lengthy waits. "These workers can't start companies, justify buying houses, or grow deep roots in their communities" during these waiting periods, writes Vivek Wadhwa, vice president of academics and innovation at Singularity University. "They could be required to leave the United States immediately—without notice—if their employer lays them off. Rather than live in constant fear and stagnate in their careers, many are returning home."

Within Congress, several proposals have been made to improve this process, including the bipartisan Startup Act 2.0, which would introduce a "startup visa" for foreign entrepreneurs who demonstrate intent to create businesses and jobs in the United States, as well as eliminate individual country visa quotas and offer a new type of visa to foreign students graduating from U.S. universities in STEM fields.

Guest worker programs for unskilled workers—particularly in the agricultural sector—have also been the subject of heated debate. Critics of the existing H-2A program, which grants temporary visas for seasonal agricultural work, say it is too costly and inflexible for farmers and has not sufficiently curbed illegal immigration. The Agricultural Job Opportunities, Benefits, and Security (AgJOBS) Act, a bill that modifies the H-2A program and allows undocumented agricultural workers to apply for green cards under certain conditions, was introduced in 2003 but has floundered in Congress.

Over the past decade, the Development, Relief, and Education for Alien Minors Act—known as the DREAM Act—has also become a significant part of the national immigration debate. The DREAM Act would provide a pathway to citizenship for undocumented youth who immigrated as children with their families to the United States. First introduced in 2001, the bill has repeatedly stalled in Congress; in late 2010, it passed the House, but failed to garner enough votes to overcome a Senate filibuster. Proponents say the act is a crucial measure for protecting undocumented youth, who did not choose to immigrate to the United States, while critics contend that it would encourage others to immigrate illegally with hopes of eventually obtaining permanent residence for their children.

In June 2012, President Obama announced that the federal government would no longer deport undocumented youths who immigrated to the United States before the age of sixteen and are younger than thirty, have been in the country for five continuous years, and have no criminal history. Under the policy, these immigrants would be eligible for two-year work permits that have no limits on how many times they can be renewed.

In 2013, a bipartisan group of senators released a comprehensive immigration reform plan that would allow those who immigrated illegally as children to apply for permanent residence in five years, regardless of their current age.

Federal-State Tensions

Several measures have been passed to handle many immigration matters at the state level, creating an uneven patchwork of standards across the country. The use of E-Verify, an electronic system used by businesses to verify employees' immigration status, varies widely across the country, as the federal government has not passed a mandate for all states to participate. More than a dozen states have mandated its use by state agencies and employers, while California has prohibited local municipalities from enforcing its use. In other states, use of E-Verify remains optional. State laws have also been passed to ease conditions for undocumented youth through granting access to instate college tuition as well as public and private sources of financial aid.

Comprehensive immigration reform . . . has in the past received some bipartisan support. But in recent years, political polarization has dimmed chances for such legislation.

Some states have attempted to pass restrictive laws aimed at curbing illegal immigration. In April 2010, Arizona passed SB 1070, a controversial law that imposes criminal punishments on undocumented immigrants and those who harbor, employ, or transport them. One provision of SB 1070 authorizes local law enforcement to stop and ask for proof of citizenship if there is "reasonable suspicion" that someone may be undocumented, an aspect of the law that pro-immigration and civil rights advocates argue has led to racial profiling. Despite harsh criticism over Arizona's law, however, several other states—including Alabama, Georgia, South Carolina, Tennessee, and Florida—have approved or considered similar legislation.

In July 2010, the federal government challenged the constitutionality of SB 1070 and the case was brought before the Supreme Court. In June 2012, the court struck down three of the four major parts of the law, including provisions that made it a state crime for undocumented immigrants to seek or perform work or fail to carry registration papers, and one provision that allowed law enforcement to arrest them without a warrant if there was "probable cause" that they committed a public offense. However, the court upheld the controversial "papers, please" provision allowing law enforcement to ask for proof of citizenship, ruling that Arizona did not overstep its state jurisdiction by enacting this portion of the law.

The immigration jurisdiction question has become a thorny issue not just in the wake of laws like SB 1070, but also as a result of policies like the Secure Communities program. Secure Communities began as a voluntary opt-in process, but when several states, unhappy with the program, attempted to opt out, their requests were denied. ICE has since stated that participation is mandatory and that the program will expand to all fifty states by 2013, eliciting protest from some local governments. To date, however, the program has not faced any legal challenges.

Outlook for Comprehensive Reform

Comprehensive immigration reform, which would improve enforcement policies and legal immigration procedures, and would offer legal status to many of the roughly eleven million undocumented immigrants living in the United States, has in the past received some bipartisan support. But in recent years, political polarization has dimmed chances for such legislation. "This issue is caught up in the political paralysis of Washington," said Angela Maria Kelley of the Center for American Progress, and it is an issue that "used to be bipartisan and now finds itself at the bottom of the heap because members can't break out of their partisan shell."

However, after Obama was reelected for a second presidential term in 2012, the White House and congressional lawmakers have made comprehensive immigration reform a high priority. In early 2013, the so-called "Gang of Eight," a group of four Democratic and four Republican senators, unveiled new immigration legislation based on months of closed-door negotiations and built on four pillars: enhancing border security, providing a pathway to citizenship for undocumented immigrants already in the country, deterring employers from hiring undocumented workers, and reforming legal immigration pathways.

The bill roughly doubles the number of H1-B visas allocated to high-skilled workers, and establishes programs for guest workers and seasonal agricultural workers. Undocumented immigrants who fit a specific set of criteria would be eligible to apply for a temporary "nonimmigrant visa" only after the borders are secured to a specific level—after which they would have to wait a minimum of ten years without federal benefits before applying for permanent residence. Young undocumented immigrants brought to the United States as children would be eligible to apply for permanent residence and citizenship after five years. If the bill passes, it will be the biggest overhaul to the U.S. immigration system in more than two decades.

The Facts Support Immigration Reform with a Path to Citizenship

Ann Garcia

Ann Garcia is a policy analyst for the Immigration Policy Team at the Center for American Progress, a progressive think tank in Washington, DC.

Below are the latest and most essential facts about immigrants and immigration reform in our nation today.

Today's Foreign-Born Immigrant Population

- *The immigrant population in the United States grew considerably over the past 50 years.* In 2011 there were 40.4 million foreign-born people residing in the United States, whereas the immigrant population in 1960 was 9.7 million. Broken down by immigration status, the foreign-born population in 2011 was composed of 15.5 million naturalized U.S. citizens, 13.1 million legal permanent residents, and 11.1 million unauthorized migrants.
- *The foreign-born share of the U.S. population has more than doubled since the 1960s but remains below historic highs.* The immigrant population was 5.4 percent of the total U.S. population in 1960, when 1 in 20 residents were foreign-born. In 2011 immigrants made up 13 percent of the total U.S. population, meaning that they were one in every eight U.S. residents. Still, today's

Ann Garcia, "The Facts on Immigration Today," Center for American Progress, April 3, 2013.

share of the immigrant population as a percentage of the total U.S. population remains below its peak in 1890, when 14.8 percent of the U.S. population had immigrated to the country.

- *Two in three immigrants living in the United States arrived before 2000.* Of the foreign-born population living in the United States in 2011, 38 percent arrived before 1990 and 27 percent arrived between 1990 and 1999.
- *The past decade saw a large increase in foreign-born migrants.* Between 2000 and 2011 there was a 30 percent increase in the foreign-born population. The immigrant population grew from 31.1 million to 40.04 million.
- *The countries of origin of today's immigrants are more diverse than they were 50 years ago.* In 1960 a full 75 percent of the foreign-born population residing in the United States came from Europe, while today only 12 percent came from Europe. In 2010 11.7 million foreign-born residents—29 percent of the foreign-born population—came from Mexico. About 2.2 million immigrants residing in the United States came from China; 1.8 million came from each India and the Philippines; 1.2 million immigrated from each Vietnam and El Salvador; and 1.1 million arrived from each Cuba and Korea.
- *Immigrants today are putting down roots across the United States, in contrast to trends we saw 50 years ago.* In the 1960s two-thirds of U.S. states had populations with less than 5 percent foreign-born individuals, but the opposite is true today. In 2010 two-thirds of states had immigrant populations above 5 percent. In 2010, 67 percent of the foreign born lived in the West and the South—a dramatic shift since the 1960s, when 70 percent of the immigrant population lived in the Northeast and Midwest.

- *Females outnumber males in the foreign-born population today.* In 2011, 51.1 percent of the U.S. immigrant population was female. Until the 1960s immigrant men outnumbered immigrant women, but by the 1970s the number of female immigrants caught up and even surpassed male immigrants. In 2011 there were 96 immigrant men arriving in America for every 100 immigrant women.
- *There are almost 1 million gay and transgender adult immigrants in the United States today.* The estimated 904,000 gay and transgender adult immigrants are more likely to be young and male compared to the overall immigrant population.
- *Immigrants have a diverse set of educational backgrounds.* About 68 percent of the foreign-born population have a high school diploma, GED, or higher, compared to 89 percent of the native-born population. Approximately 11 percent of immigrants have a master's degree, professional degree, or doctorate, compared to 10.2 percent of the native-born population.
- *More than half of the foreign born are homeowners.* Around 52 percent of immigrants own their own homes, compared to 67 percent of native-born individuals. Among immigrants, 66 percent of naturalized citizens own their homes.
- *The 20 million U.S.-born children of immigrants are significantly better off financially than their immigrant parents.* The median annual household income of second-generation adult Americans is $58,100, just $100 shy of the national average. This is significantly higher than their parents' median annual household income of $45,800.

- *U.S.-born children of immigrants are more likely to go to college, less likely to be living in poverty, and equally likely to be homeowners as the average American.* About 36 percent of U.S.-born children of immigrants are college graduates—5 percent above the national average. Around 64 percent of them are homeowners—just 1 percent under the national average. And 11 percent of U.S.-born children of immigrants are in poverty—well below the national average of 13 percent.

The Undocumented Immigrant Population

- *The growth of the undocumented immigrant population has slowed in recent years.* In 2000 there were an estimated 8.4 million undocumented persons residing in the United States. This population peaked in 2007 at 12 million, but decreased to 11.1 million by 2009 and remains stable at 11.1 million in 2011.

- *People from Mexico account for a large part of the undocumented population living in the United States.* 6.8 million people, or 59 percent of the undocumented population, are from Mexico. Another 6 percent of the undocumented population is from El Salvador; 5 percent is from Guatemala; 3 percent is from Honduras; and 2 percent is from China and the Philippines.

- *The majority of undocumented immigrants are well-settled in the United States.* About 63 percent of undocumented immigrants had been living in the United States for 10 years or longer in 2010.

- *Undocumented immigrants are often part of the same family as documented immigrants.* 16.6 million people were in "mixed status" families—those with at least one undocumented immigrant in 2010. Nine million of these families have at least one U.S.-born child.

- *Undocumented immigrants are more likely than native-born Americans to be rearing children.* About 46 percent of undocumented immigrants, or about 4.7 million people, were part of families with children in 2008. By comparison, the figure for U.S. native adults and documented immigrants who live in families with children is 29 percent and 38 percent, respectively.

- *Millions of U.S.-citizen children have undocumented parents.* 4.5 million U.S.-born children had at least one unauthorized immigrant parent in 2010, an increase from 2.1 million in 2000.

- *There are more than a quarter of a million gay and transgender undocumented adult immigrants in the United States today.* The estimated 267,000 gay and transgender undocumented adult immigrants are more likely to be male and younger relative to all undocumented immigrants. Around 71 percent of undocumented gay and transgender adults are Hispanic, and 15 percent are Asian American or Pacific Islander.

- *Nearly half of settled undocumented immigrants are homeowners.* Among undocumented immigrants who had lived in the United States for 10 years or longer, 45 percent were homeowners in 2008. Among undocumented immigrants who have lived here for less than 10 years, 27 percent were homeowners in 2008.

- *Undocumented immigrants comprise a disproportionately large percent of the labor force relative to their numbers.* About 5.2 percent of the U.S. labor force consisted of undocumented immigrants in 2010, even though they comprised only 3.7 percent of the U.S. population.

- *More than half of the undocumented immigrant population has a high school degree or higher.* 52 percent of undocumented immigrants had a high school diploma or higher in 2008, and 15 percent have a bachelor's degree or higher. . . .

Immigrants and the Economy

- *Permitting undocumented immigrants to earn citizenship would significantly expand economic growth.* If the currently undocumented population were granted legal status in 2013 and citizenship five years later, the 10-year cumulative increase in U.S. GDP would be $1.1 trillion.
- *Granting legal status and citizenship to undocumented immigrants would create jobs and increase tax revenues.* If undocumented immigrants acquired legal status in 2013 and citizenship five years later, they would create an average of 159,000 jobs per year, and they would pay an additional $144 billion in federal, state, and local taxes over a 10-year period.
- *Legalization and naturalization of undocumented immigrants would bolster wages.* The annual income of the unauthorized would be 15.1 percent higher within five years if they were granted legal status starting in 2013. If undocumented immigrants earned their citizenship five years after receiving legal status, their wages would be an additional 10 percent higher. This means that by 2022 the wages of today's undocumented population could be 25.1 percent higher than they are today.
- *Immigration reform that includes legalizing the undocumented population would yield huge gains in gross domestic product.* Immigration reform that would legalize the approximately 11 million individuals who currently lack papers in the United States would add a cumulative $1.5 trillion to U.S. gross domestic product, or GDP, over 10 years.

- *Undocumented immigrants pay billions in taxes annually.* Households headed by unauthorized immigrants paid $11.2 billion in state and local taxes in 2010. Immigrants—even legal immigrants—are barred from most social services, meaning that they pay to support benefits they cannot even receive.
- *Contrary to common fears, immigrants are not in direct competition with native-born American workers in part because they tend to have different skill sets.* The research shows that American workers are not harmed by—and may even benefit—from immigration because immigrants tend to be complementary workers, helping Americans be more productive.
- *Passage of the DREAM Act would inject billions of dollars into the American economy while creating more than a million jobs.* The DREAM Act would provide a pathway to legal status for eligible young people who complete high school and some college or military service. Approximately $329 billion and 1.4 million jobs would be added to the American economy over the next two decades if the DREAM Act became law. Passing the DREAM Act would also increase federal revenue by $10 billion.
- *The economic gains that stem from legalizing of the undocumented population would also be reflected at the state level.* Gains in selected states are as follows:
    - *Arizona*: Total wages would increase by $1.8 billion if the 400,000 undocumented immigrants living in Arizona were legalized. The state would also gain $540 million in tax revenue, and 39,000 jobs would be created.
    - *Florida*: Total wages would increase by $3.8 billion if the 825,000 undocumented immigrants living in

Florida were legalized. The state would also gain $1.13 billion in tax revenue, and 97,000 jobs would be created.

- *Texas*: Total wages would increase by $9.7 billion if the 1,650,000 undocumented immigrants living in Texas were legalized. The state would also gain $4.1 billion in tax revenue, and 193,000 jobs would be created.

The Costs of Deportation

- *A "self-deportation" regime would cost our economy trillions of dollars.* If all undocumented immigrants in the country were deported or were to "self-deport"—meaning they choose to leave the country because life is too difficult—the United States cumulative gross domestic product would suffer a hit of $2.6 trillion over 10 years.

- *Mass deportation of the undocumented immigrant population would cost taxpayers hundreds of billions of dollars.* Deporting the entire undocumented population would cost $285 billion over a five-year period, including continued border and interior enforcement efforts. For that price, we could hire more than 1 million new public high school teachers, and pay their salaries for five years.

- *It costs taxpayers more than $20,000 to carry out the deportation of a single individual.* Apprehending, detaining, processing, and transporting one individual in the deportation process cost $23,482 in fiscal year 2008.

- *The cost of mass deportation policy would also be reflected in economic losses at the state level.* Costs to selected states are as follows:

- *Arizona*: Deporting the 400,000 undocumented immigrants living in Arizona would cost the state $13.3 billion in lost gross state product. The state coffers would take a hit of $2.4 billion in tax revenue, and there would be a $6.25 billion decrease in total wages.
- *Florida*: Deporting the 825,000 undocumented immigrants living in Florida would cost the state $31.22 billion in lost gross state product. The state coffers would take a hit of $5.67 billion in tax revenue, and there would be a $15.45 billion decrease in total wages.
- *Texas*: Deporting the 1,650,000 undocumented immigrants living in Texas would cost the state $77.7 billion in lost gross state product. The state coffers would take a hit of $14.5 billion in tax revenue, and there would be a $33.2 billion decrease in total wages.

Our Borders Are More Secure than Ever Before

- *Five years after the border-security benchmarks were written into the 2007 Comprehensive Immigration Reform Act, all targets have been hit or surpassed*:
    - *Border agents*: 21,370 Border Patrol agents patrol the borders—1,370 higher than the goal set in 2007—and 1,200 National Guard troops are on the ground.
    - *Fencing*: 651 total miles of fencing have been built along the southwest border, just one mile shy of what the Secure Fence Act of 2006 mandates.
    - *Surveillance*: 179 mobile video surveillance systems and 168 radar and camera towers have been in-

stalled—more than was required in the 2007 benchmarks. The increase in unmanned aircraft systems and mobile surveillance systems surpassed the 2007 goals by 2 and 47, respectively.

- *Increased consequences*: Resources are available to detain 1,300 more people per day than the 2007 goal set out to meet. The Border Patrol ended the process of "catch and release," a practice where two of every three apprehended border crossers from outside of Mexico were released into the United States pending removal hearings. The Department of Homeland Security instead expanded the "consequence delivery system," to the entire border. This system steps up criminal penalties for people caught illegally crossing the border, and often returns immigrants to unfamiliar and far-away border cities in an effort to cut the migrant off from the smuggler who helped with their previous border-crossing attempt.
- "*Operational control*": 81 percent of the U.S. border with Mexico meets one of the Department of Homeland Security's three highest standards of security: controlled, managed, or monitored. The remaining sections of the border are in the most inaccessible and inhospitable areas of the border. 67 Total control of the border is impossible, but Customs and Border Protection continues to make great strides in gaining control of important sectors.
- *The number of people apprehended crossing the border has decreased to the lowest level in 40 years.* Even though border agents now patrol every mile of the U.S. border daily, and in many places they can view nearly all attempts to cross the border in

real time, 27 percent fewer individuals were apprehended in 2011 than in 2010.

- *Net undocumented migration from Mexico is now at or below zero.* Heightened border enforcement and a worsening U.S. job market together have caused a sharp drop in unauthorized migration from Mexico to the United States. In the future we can expect that improved Mexican economic conditions and falling birth rates in Mexico will continue this trend, even as the American economy recovers from the Great Recession.
- *A clear path to citizenship for the approximately 11 million undocumented immigrants and a 21st century legal immigration system that meets our economy's needs will ease our border security burdens in the future.* When immigrants have a legal, practicable, and less onerous way to come into this country to live and work, they will not need to enter the United States by illicitly crossing our borders.

Immigration Enforcement Is in Overdrive

- *President Obama's administration deported 1.5 million immigrants during his first term in office.* In fiscal year 2012, 409,849 people were deported. Though 96 percent of deportations fell under the Immigration and Customs Enforcement "priority removals" category, the total number of deportations last year sets a record high in the United States.
- *The average daily population of immigrant detainees being held has increased by 1,000 detainees per fiscal year since 2007.* On average, Immigration and Customs Enforcement detained 34,069 people on any given day in fiscal year 2012. Keeping these individuals in detention

while proper authorities determine their fates costs taxpayers roughly $2 million a day, and the average detainee spent 26.5 days in detention in fiscal year 2012.

- *In 2011 at least 5,100 citizen children of undocumented immigrants were living in foster care because their parents were detained or deported.* An estimated 200,000 parents of children who are U.S. citizens were deported between 2010 and 2012. If the rules are not changed, 15,000 more children will face a similar fate by 2016.
- *The Department of Homeland Security's immigration enforcement program—Secure Communities—is active in 97 percent of jurisdictions.* The Secure Communities program checks the immigration status of those booked into county jails in participating jurisdictions. It was expanded from 14 jurisdictions in 2008 to 3,074 jurisdictions in 2012, but several states and cities such as Washington, D.C., Illinois, and New York have expressed concerns that the program interferes with local policing priorities, and inevitably leads to racial profiling.
- *Until we legalize the currently undocumented population, E-Verify will not help break the jobs magnet that leads many to immigrate without legal status.* E-Verify, an online system to check an employee's work authorization status, is currently used by 409,000 businesses in the United States. But the program contains significant flaws, including failing to accurately identify unauthorized immigrants 54 percent of the time. If the program became mandatory for all employers today, it would cause 770,000 legally present and legally authorized workers to lose their jobs. Even if E-Verify was fine-tuned, expanding the program to cover all employers could only work in concert with a legalization pro-

gram that allows the 5 percent of the labor force currently in the shadows to come out and work legally.

- *The federal government has stepped up enforcement against employers who hire undocumented workers by auditing I-9 forms.* All workers and employers upon hiring an employee must complete this federal paperwork. Immigration and Customs Enforcement conducted more than 3,000 worksite audits in fiscal year 2012, up from the 2,496 in the previous fiscal year, and from the 503 that were carried out in fiscal year 2008.

The Senate's Proposed Immigration Reform Will Shrink the Deficit and Grow the US Economy

Doug Elmendorf

Doug Elmendorf, an economist, is the director of the Congressional Budget Office, a federal research agency charged with providing economic data and analysis to the US Congress.

The Border Security, Economic Opportunity, and Immigration Modernization Act (S. 744) would revise laws governing immigration and the enforcement of those laws, allowing for a significant increase in the number of noncitizens who could lawfully enter the United States on both a permanent and temporary basis. Additionally, the bill would create a process for many individuals who are present in the country now on an unauthorized basis to gain legal status, subject to requirements specified in the bill. The bill also would directly appropriate funds for tightening border security and enforcing immigration laws, and would authorize future appropriations for those purposes.

Based on joint work with the staff of the Joint Committee on Taxation (JCT), CBO [Congressional Budget Office, a federal agency that provides economic information to the US Congress] released two analyses related to the immigration legislation that was approved by the Senate Judiciary Committee:

- A cost estimate providing projections of the bill's effects on federal spending, revenues, and the deficit.

Doug Elmendorf, "CBO Releases Two Analyses of the Senate's Immigration Legislation," Congressional Budget Office, June 18, 2013.

- A report on the economic impact of S. 744, analyzing the bill's effects on economic output, the size of the labor force, employment, wages, capital investment, interest rates, and productivity.

How Would the Legislation Affect the U.S. Population?

CBO estimates that, by 2023, enacting S. 744 would lead to a net increase of 10.4 million in the number of people residing in the United States, compared with the number projected under current law. That increase would grow to about 16 million by 2033. CBO also estimates that about 8 million unauthorized residents would initially gain legal status under the bill, but that change in status would not affect the size of the U.S. population.

How Would the Legislation Affect the Federal Budget from 2014 Through 2023?

CBO and JCT estimate that enacting S. 744 would generate changes in direct spending and revenues that would decrease federal budget deficits by $197 billion over the 2014–2023 period. CBO also estimates that implementing the legislation would result in net discretionary costs of $22 billion over the 2014–2023 period, assuming appropriation of the amounts authorized or otherwise needed to implement the legislation. Combining those figures would lead to a net savings of about $175 billion over the 2014–2023 period from enacting S. 744. However, the net impact of the bill on federal deficits would depend on future actions by lawmakers, who could choose to appropriate more or less than the amounts estimated by CBO. In addition, the total amount of discretionary funding is currently capped (through 2021) by the Budget Control Act of 2011; extra funding for the purposes of this legislation might lead to lower funding for other purposes.

Following the long-standing convention of not incorporating macroeconomic effects in cost estimates—a practice that has been followed in the Congressional budget process since it was established in 1974—cost estimates produced by CBO and JCT typically reflect the assumption that macroeconomic variables such as gross domestic product (GDP) and employment remain fixed at the values they are projected to reach under current law. However, because S. 744 would significantly increase the size of the U.S. labor force, CBO and JCT relaxed that assumption by incorporating in this cost estimate their projections of the direct effects of the bill on the U.S. population, employment, and taxable compensation.

The bill also would have a broader set of effects on output and income that are not reflected in the cost estimate described above. Those additional economic effects include changes in the productivity of labor and capital, the income earned by capital, the rate of return on capital (and therefore the interest rate on government debt), and the differences in wages for workers with different skills. Those effects and their estimated consequences for the federal budget are described in a report, "*The Economic Impact of S. 744, the Border Security, Economic Opportunity, and Immigration Modernization*" that accompanies the cost estimate.

S. 744 would boost economic output. Taking account of all economic effects . . . the bill would increase real (inflation-adjusted) GDP relative to the amount CBO projects under current law by 3.3 percent in 2023 and by 5.4 percent in 2033.

According to CBO's central estimates (within a range that reflects the uncertainty about two key economic relationships in CBO's analysis), the economic impacts *not* included in the cost estimate would have no further net effect on budget deficits over the 2014–2023 period.

How Would the Legislation Affect the Federal Budget for 2024 Through 2033?

CBO and JCT generally do not provide cost estimates beyond the standard 10-year projection period. However, S. 744 would cause a significant number of people to become eligible for certain federal benefits in the decade following 2023, so CBO and JCT have extended their estimate of the effects of this legislation for another decade.

The additional amount of federal direct spending stemming from enactment of S. 744 would grow after 2023 as more people became eligible for federal benefits as a result of the bill. The additional amount of federal revenues owing to the legislation also would increase after 2023 as the labor force continued to increase. On balance, CBO and JCT estimate that those changes in direct spending and revenues would decrease federal budget deficits by about $700 billion (or 0.2 percent of total output) over the 2024–2033 period. In addition, the legislation would have a net discretionary cost of $20 billion to $25 billion over the 2024–2033 period, assuming appropriation of the necessary amounts. According to CBO's central estimates (within a range that reflects the uncertainty about two key economic relationships in CBO's analysis), the economic impacts not included in the cost estimate would further reduce deficits (relative to the effects reported in the cost estimate) by about $300 billion over the 2024–2033 period.

How Would the Legislation Affect the Economy?

S. 744 would boost economic output. Taking account of all economic effects (including those reflected in the cost estimate), the bill would increase real (inflation-adjusted) GDP [gross domestic product, a measure of the country's total economic output] relative to the amount CBO projects under current law by 3.3 percent in 2023 and by 5.4 percent in

2033, according to CBO's central estimates. Compared with GDP, gross national product (GNP) per capita accounts for the effect on incomes of international capital flows and adjusts for the number of people in the country. Relative to what would occur under current law, S. 744 would lower per capita GNP by 0.7 percent in 2023 and raise it by 0.2 percent in 2033, according to CBO's central estimates.

Per capita GNP would be less than 1 percent lower than under current law through 2031 because the increase in the population would be greater, proportionately, than the increase in output; after 2031, however, the opposite would be true. CBO's central estimates also show that average wages for the entire labor force would be 0.1 percent *lower* in 2023 and 0.5 percent *higher* in 2033 under the legislation than under current law. Average wages would be slightly lower than under current law through 2024, primarily because the amount of capital available to workers would not increase as rapidly as the number of workers and because the new workers would be less skilled and have lower wages, on average, than the labor force under current law. However, the rate of return on capital would be higher under the legislation than under current law throughout the next two decades.

The estimated reductions in average wages and per capita GNP for much of the next two decades do not necessarily imply that current U.S. residents would be worse off, on average, under the legislation than they would be under current law. Both of those figures represent differences between the averages for *all* U.S. residents under the legislation—including both the people who would be residents under current law and the additional people who would come to the country under the legislation—and the averages under current law for people who would be residents in the absence of the legislation. As noted, the additional people who would become residents under the legislation would earn lower wages, on average, than other residents, which would pull down the average wage and per capita GNP; at the same time, the income earned by capital would increase. CBO has not analyzed the full economic effects of the legislation separately for the incomes of people who would be U.S. residents under current law.

In sum, relative to current law, enacting S. 744 would:

- Increase the size of the labor force and employment,
- Increase average wages in 2025 and later years (but decrease them before that),
- Slightly raise the unemployment rate through 2020,
- Boost the amount of capital investment,
- Raise the productivity of labor and of capital, and
- Result in higher interest rates.

Proposed Immigration Reforms Will Bring More Highly Skilled Workers into the US Economy

Marco Rubio

Marco Rubio is a US Republican senator from Florida.

Today [May 8, 2013], the U.S. Senate Committee on Commerce, Science & Transportation will examine the role of immigrants in America's innovation economy. More specifically, the committee will look at how our broken immigration system is holding back American innovation and job creation, and how the immigration reform proposal before the Senate can promote a thriving U.S. technology sector that benefits American workers.

Attracting Educated, Skilled Workers

While there are a number of broken aspects of our immigration system today—including porous borders, weak workplace enforcement and an inadequate system to track foreign visitors who overstay their visas—one that also stands out is the way we handle academic talent and highly skilled workers.

Every year, our colleges and universities graduate thousands of foreign students who have been educated in our world-class university system. But instead of putting that talent to work in the American economy, we send them home to places like China and India to compete against us. In other words, in many cases, other nations end up benefitting more from our education system than the United States does.

Marco Rubio, "America Needs A Pro-Growth Immigration System," *Tech Crunch*, May 8, 2013.

The Senate immigration reform bill would end this debacle. After educating the world's brightest and most innovative minds, we will no longer send them home; we will instead staple green cards to their diplomas.

We will also expand the highly skilled H1-B visa program from the current 65,000 to a program with a new floor of 110,000, a ceiling of 180,000, and an additional 25,000 exemptions for persons who graduate from a U.S. university with an advanced degree in science, technology, engineering or math. In order to accomplish these necessary moves to a more merit-based immigration system, we eliminate certain categories of family preferences that have allowed for chain migration and completely eliminate the diversity visa lottery, among other reforms.

A Benefit for the Economy and Budget

These measures, which we hope to improve on as the bill moves through the legislative process, are at the heart of our efforts to modernize our legal immigration system to help meet the needs of our 21st century economy, make it more merit and skill-based than ever, and allow our economy to remain a dynamic global leader. They are also the kinds of reforms that will make immigration reform a net benefit for our economy and our federal budget—the way immigration has always been a net benefit for America.

Let there be no doubt that immigration will always be a powerful source of American strength.

For example, studies show that 40 percent of American Fortune 500 firms were started by immigrants, as are roughly half of the most successful startups in Silicon Valley. This doesn't just lead to corner-office, executive-level jobs; these generate jobs across the income spectrum that help Americans rise to the middle class and beyond.

With the reforms being offered, the benefits to our economy and our people will come from the infusion of entrepreneurs, innovators, investors, skilled workers and others driven by the desire to build a better life for themselves and their children. And when our economy needs foreign workers to fill labor shortages, our modernized system will ensure that the future flow of workers is manageable, traceable, fair to American workers, and in line with our economy's needs.

Let there be no doubt that immigration will always be a powerful source of American strength. While some worry that the immigrants that will most benefit from the Senate's legislation are mostly poor, with limited education and destined to be government dependents, history has proven something else. It has demonstrated the power of the American free enterprise system to lift people from the circumstances of their birth and into more prosperous and stable lives for themselves and their children. Over two centuries of life in America have demonstrated this to be true.

A Broken Immigration System

Of course, there are legitimate questions some have raised about why this is now the Senate's priority. During the time I've been working on immigration reform legislation, I've been asked why we are dealing with this issue at this time, with some questioning the need of dealing with it at all with so many other pressing concerns like our growing debt, millions of unemployed or underemployed Americans, and the persistent threat of terrorism that recently manifested itself on our soil.

It's absolutely true that these are the defining issues of our time that, frankly, should have been addressed a long time ago.

But the reality of immigration in America today is that, even if we didn't have some 11 million illegal immigrants in the U.S. today, we would still have to fix our broken legal immigration system.

The immigration system we have today is a disaster. It's de facto amnesty that threatens our security and our sovereignty. But even worse, it's a job killer.

The immigration proposal being considered by the Senate is not perfect. And I believe we can improve it with the ideas of people like [Senator] Orrin Hatch who care deeply about fixing the immigration system to work better for American workers.

As the immigration debate continues, it is important that we use today's hearing and every other avenue we have to fix the broken immigration system we have. In doing so, we can move towards a strong, effective system that will secure the border, encourage job creation for Americans, and ensure America remains a dynamic global economic leader.

Just and Humane Immigration Reform Will Bring Immigrants Out of the Shadows

Timothy Dolan

Timothy Dolan, a cardinal in the Catholic Church, is archbishop of New York and president of the US Conference of Catholic Bishops.

Immigration reform is an issue close to Catholic hearts. America has wonderfully welcomed generations of immigrant families, and our parishes, schools and charitable ministries have long helped successfully integrate immigrants into American life.

Congress will soon debate the most comprehensive overhaul of our nation's immigration laws in almost 30 years. With the stakes so high, it's important that Congress craft legislation that balances the legitimate needs of security with our heritage of welcoming immigrants and the gifts they bring to our country.

Practical and Humane Immigration Reform

We bishops call for practical and humane immigration reform grounded in the Catholic experience. All around the country, parishes and service groups help immigrants through English classes, job training, medical aid and other basic assistance. Catholic Charities agencies alone provided services to 400,000 immigrants last year. With this hand of welcome, we help newly-arrived migrants integrate into our communities.

We also see up close the suffering caused by the broken immigration system. Our nation has deported more than 1.5

Timothy Dolan, "Catholic Bishops: Fix Unjust Immigration System," *USA Today*, June 9, 2013.

million people over the past five years, separating hundreds of thousands of parents from their U.S.-citizen children. Our detention system has exploded, incarcerating 400,000 a year, often in substandard conditions. And our brothers and sisters continue to die horrible deaths on both sides of the border. In 2012, the remains of 129 migrants were found in one Texas county alone.

Such fundamental humanitarian problems require a response. While addressing this complex problem raises tough questions about which good people can disagree, Americans have always brought faith to bear on public issues, and Biblical teachings provide principles to guide us. Given these teachings and experience, we've called for an earned path to citizenship to bring a generous number of people out of the shadows in a reasonable amount of time.

We also believe that family unity, based on the union of a husband and a wife and their children, must be a cornerstone of immigration reform, because strong families are the foundation of the robust communities that integrate immigrants into American life. Poor and low-skilled workers should be able to enter the country legally and safely; the integrity of our borders should be assured; and due process protections should be restored to our system, including alternatives to detention. Given the desperate situations from which migrants flee, our foreign policy must address the root economic and social causes of migration.

The Senate proposal, while not perfect, goes a long way toward correcting injustices in the system. Despite its shortcomings, the bill significantly improves upon the status quo and will assist millions of families. We look forward to continuing to work with Congress to improve the legislation, and we applaud lawmakers of both parties who are working together to bring 11 million people out of the shadows.

In the end, immigration reform is about answers to some basic questions. How do we treat our brothers and sisters? Do we want to continue a system that keeps millions of people in a permanent underclass? Do we want to continue to separate a generation of children from their parents? Do we want to continue the American heritage of hospitality or not? We must do better.

The late Ed Koch, the former mayor of New York, once told me that immigrants to New York knew they were welcome because of two great figures: the Statue of Liberty and the Catholic Church. I'm proud to be pastor of an archdiocese that has served generations of immigrants. And I'm humbled to know that at this moment we're called to live up to the best of that history. When the grandchildren of today's immigrants look back on this moment, let them see America at its best—welcoming, generous and openhearted.

The Senate's Proposed Immigration Reform Reinforces Failed Immigration Policies

Rosemary Jenks

Rosemary Jenks is director of government relations for NumbersUSA, an organization that works to stabilize the size of the US population and reduce immigration numbers.

The Schumer-Rubio amnesty bill passed out of the Senate Judiciary Committee last week [May 21, 2013] doesn't reform our broken immigration system so much as it doubles down on the failed policies that got us here.

The bill guarantees amnesty now in exchange for promises of future enforcement, just like the failed 1986 amnesty. In addition to inviting the next wave of illegal immigration, though, the bill would double legal immigration and vastly expand guest worker programs for both low- and high-skilled foreign workers. It is a recipe for sustained high unemployment, ever-expanding government, and fiscal deficits.

Breaking Promises

The Gang of Eight Senators (Schumer, Rubio, McCain, Durbin, Graham, Menendez, Flake, and Bennet) wants us to trust that this bill will end illegal immigration and make America more prosperous. That's asking a lot, considering that the bill breaks every promise the Gang has made to America.

Gangster Rubio promised the "toughest enforcement measures in the history of the country." Instead, the bill requires a plan for 90 percent effective border control, as measured by the Secretary of the Department of Homeland Security (DHS), who insists the border is already secure. It actually weakens current law, which requires a biometric entry-and-exit system at all ports of entry—land, air, and sea—by requiring only a biographic system at air and sea ports. It also fails to quickly implement a mandatory employment-verification program, instead dragging the process out at least five years, exempting some employers altogether, and giving the DHS Secretary the discretion to scuttle the whole system.

Gangster Graham promised the bill would "make situations like Boston less likely to happen." That's interesting considering that the bill actually loosens asylum rules and lengthens the appeal process for illegal aliens denied asylum. It also eviscerates the ability of Immigration and Customs Enforcement (ICE) officers to detain and deport future illegal aliens—including potential terrorists and criminals—by prohibiting ICE from detaining aliens unless they prove there is no alternative to detention and by giving the DHS Secretary and immigration judges almost total discretion to let immigration lawbreakers remain here.

The [Senate immigration reform] bill is a huge bonanza for special interests . . . but it is a disaster for American sovereignty and for American workers and taxpayers.

Gangster Schumer promised the bill "will pay for itself" and not cost taxpayers a dime. Call me crazy, but I'm more inclined to believe Heritage's Robert Rector, whose research shows that the net cost of amnesty alone (not including the bill's massive increase in low-skilled immigration) will be $6.3 trillion, rather than Chuck Schumer and his fellow gangsters.

Gangster Flake promised amnestied aliens would have to "pay all back taxes" to get green cards. Not only does the bill not require amnestied aliens to pay all back taxes, it doesn't require the employers who paid them off the books to pay back taxes. Even more egregious, the bill allows amnestied aliens to qualify for the refundable Earned Income Tax Credit and the Additional Child Tax Credit—to the tune of $10 billion a year, according to Heritage. This means that when amnestied aliens do actually have to start paying taxes, we will be giving them a check.

Gangster Rubio promised the bill will "moderniz[e] our legal immigration system." Rather than considering legal immigration based on what is in the national interest, though, the bill proposes a system that would grant 33 million green cards in the next decade alone—that's more than were granted over the four decades between 1972 and 2012. On top of that, the bill would bring in millions more guest workers, plus their families. Meanwhile, unemployment is almost 8 percent, more than 20 million Americans can't find full-time work, and the labor force participation rate is lower than it has been since women began joining the workforce in large numbers. Apparently, the Gang sees nothing wrong with paying Americans to remain unemployed while we transform America by importing millions of foreign workers to compete for scarce jobs and suppress the wages of working Americans.

The Schumer-Rubio bill is a huge bonanza for special interests—employers seeking cheap labor, unions seeking to increase dues, ethnic-identity groups seeking to expand their influence, immigration lawyers seeking clients, illegal aliens, and liberals seeking to expand the government and their voting bloc—but it is a disaster for American sovereignty and for American workers and taxpayers.

Comprehensive Immigration Reform Will Not Fix Our Immigration System

James Carafano

James Carafano is the director of the Allison Center for Foreign Policy Studies, a project of The Heritage Foundation, a conservative think tank in Washington, DC.

The good news is Congress cares about trying to fix our flawed immigration system and broken borders.

The bad news is they want to do it with a solution that looks a lot like Obamacare [the health-care legislation signed by President Barack Obama]—the "Gang of Eight" 844-page-plus comprehensive bill.

The sad news is that such an "easy button" solution will not improve our immigration system.

A Failed Bill

History shows that big bills designed to solve everything wind up creating as many problems as they address. They become loaded with payoffs for special interests and often introduce measures that work at cross purposes.

The "comprehensive" bill fails at the start. Here are the top five reasons it cannot be fixed.

1. Amnesty. This bill grants amnesty. It creates a framework for legalization for the estimated 11 million people unlawfully present in the United States. Anyone who was present in the U.S. before 2012 qualifies, but there is too much opportunity for fraud—since there is no proof required that applicants have been here for several years.

James Carafano, "Morning Bell: Top 5 Problems with the 'Comprehensive' Immigration Bill," The Foundry, April 23, 2013.

2. Fiscal Costs to the Taxpayer. This plan does not account for the government benefits, especially welfare and entitlement benefits, that would be paid to those who are legalized over their lifetimes. The additional costs to taxpayers would be enormous. Some argue that amnesty would bring economic gains, but these would actually be captured by the formerly unlawful immigrants themselves. Legalization brings little economic benefit to the rest of us.

3. Government Spending. The bill is a Trojan horse for government spending, and in some cases, it appears the funding is unrestricted or ill-defined. Just one example is a $6.5 billion "Comprehensive Immigration Reform Trust," which includes a $2 billion "slush fund" for border security.

Our federal government currently spends $1 trillion more per year than it takes in, so adding on a new, unlimited spending commitment makes no sense at all. The entire cost of implementing the bill has yet to be determined. Further, the bill trashes fiscal discipline, exploiting a loophole in the Budget Control Act (BCA) that allows Congress to spend more than allowed under the spending caps adopted in 2011.

Just throwing money at the border does not make sense. The policies adopted on both sides of the border are more important.

---

4. "Border Triggers." The bill requires certification of "border triggers" for stemming the tide of illegal border crossings before additional steps in the legalization process can proceed.

But the Department of Homeland Security has been trying unsuccessfully to define credible metrics for border security since 2004. Even if it had effective "triggers," that does not guarantee a secure border. Border crossing conditions constantly change. Even if the goal is achieved, there is no guarantee it will stay that way.

Amnesty creates an incentive for illegal border crossings and overstays. Thus, the strategy laid out would drive up the cost of securing the border. Just throwing money at the border does not make sense. The policies adopted on both sides of the border are more important.

For example, the Coast Guard is significantly underfunded and unprepared. America's coastlines are already seeing a significant increase in illegal entry by sea, a trend that has been growing since 2007.

5. *Lawful Immigration Reform.* The bill "modernizes" lawful immigration and non-immigration visas. These modernizations include substantially lowering "chain" migration; abolishing the diversity lottery; expanding the visa waiver; increasing high-skill migration; and expanding temporary worker programs.

We deserve better—all of us. . . . In fact, all who cherish a society that is committed to keeping America both a nation of immigrants and a country that respects its laws deserve better.

The Way Forward

Reforming the legal immigration system—in principle—is laudable. But trying to craft precise measures in a massive bill like this is difficult. For example, though it sounds innocuous, one provision in the legislation could lead to big problems. The legislation allows documents "issued by a federally recognized Indian tribe" to be used for identity and employment purposes. Numerous Indian tribes exist along the southern border, including the Texas Kickapoo, the Ysleta Del Sur, and, the largest, the Tohona O'Odham. Indian reservations already serve as drug pipelines and have been cited as weak links in border security. Given these issues, does it really make sense to add this exemption to legislation aimed at minimizing identification fraud?

Once we get it right, there is strong bipartisan support that modernizing lawful immigration ought to be a priority. Congress should put its effort into accomplishing that aim—moving forward on an area of strong agreement, while allowing time to debate issues where there is not strong consensus.

We deserve better—all of us. Employers deserve better than having to sift through falsified credentials or risk breaking the law. Families in communities burdened by the impacts of illegal immigration deserve better. In fact, all who cherish a society that is committed to keeping America both a nation of immigrants and a country that respects its laws deserve better.

Immigration reform can move forward on many fronts at the same time, focusing on some commonsense initiatives that begin to address the practical challenges of our immigration system. The key is to begin by working on the solutions on which we can all agree, rather than insisting on a comprehensive approach that divides us.

Immigration Reform Will Not Solve the Problem of Declining Cheap Labor from Mexico

Daniel B. Wood

Daniel B. Wood is a staff writer for the Christian Science Monitor, *an international news organization and website.*

Two recent studies suggest that the immigration reform bill now making its way through the US Senate may not be able to solve one of the core long-term challenges it seeks to fix.

Beyond the weighty issues of border security and a path to citizenship for undocumented immigrants, the reform bill also targets America's migrant labor system, which both workers' rights groups and the agricultural industry say is broken. Agricultural businesses say there is not enough flexibility in the system to meet their employment needs, while workers say they can be trapped in unfair conditions.

Long-Term Changes in Mexican Cheap Labor

Both sides say the reform measure, while not perfect, is an improvement. Yet the two recent studies suggest that economic and demographic trends in Mexico are already changing the dynamics of the American migrant-worker system. In the longer term, the increasing urbanization and prosperity of the Mexican middle class will dramatically diminish the abun-

Daniel B. Wood, "Immigration Reform Too Late to Fix One Big Problem, Studies Say," *Christian Science Monitor*, May 10, 2013.

dant, very cheap Mexican farm labor that has flooded across the southern border for decades to harvest the crops of America.

"The longstanding assumption that the region has an endless supply of less-educated workers headed for the US is becoming less and less accurate when it comes to Mexico; and in the years ahead, it is also likely to become less accurate first for El Salvador and then Guatemala," says the executive summary of the report released Monday [May 6, 2013] by the Migration Policy Institute and the Woodrow Wilson International Center for Scholars.

The second study agrees with the first and connects the trend directly to issues at the heart of immigration reform.

"This [trend] means that immigration policy will cease to be a solution to the US farm labor problem in the long run and probably sooner. In fact, we already may be witnessing the start of a new era in which farmers will have to adapt to labor scarcity by switching to less labor-intensive crops, technologies, and labor management practices," according to the University of California study released in March [2013].

Together, the two studies reinforce statistically what experts have been cataloging anecdotally since the 1980s, pointing to several reasons for the historic drop in cheap Mexican farm labor.

- As incomes in Mexico have risen, workers have shifted out of farm work into other sectors. Mexico's farm workforce fell by nearly 2 million—25 percent—from 1995 to 2010, and its per capita income now exceeds $15,000 per year. "Moving away from farm work as your income rises, reflects a pattern seen in many other countries," says Eduard Taylor, one of the authors of the University of California report.

- Fertility rates have changed dramatically—down from a norm of seven children per woman in 1970 to just over two today.
- Rural education has also improved dramatically. The average schooling for rural Mexicans 50 or older is 4.9 years, but for those in their 20s it is 9.7 years. "Better educated children eschew farm work in Mexico," says Mr. Taylor.

Effects on US Immigration and Agriculture

These developments could help proponents of immigration reform dull some criticism of the plan.

American agriculture's reliance on low-wage foreign labor has impeded capital investment in technology that would have made it more efficient and competitive.

"This study suggests that the level of illegal immigration will never return to its prior levels," says Steven Schier, a political scientist at Carleton College in Northfield, Minn., referring to the University of California research. "That may serve to reduce the heat surrounding the issue and prompt Washington to address the problem with legislation for the first time in decades."

But groups against immigration say the studies show the need to focus on other ways of getting US food harvested.

"American agriculture's reliance on low-wage foreign labor has impeded capital investment in technology that would have made it more efficient and competitive," says Ira Mehlman, national spokesman for the Federation of American Immigration Reform. "There are machines that can do many agricultural jobs much more efficiently and more cost effectively. Our government should have policies in place that incentivize that sort of capital investment in efficiency, not policies that perpetuate exploitative inefficiency."

More broadly, the research helps clarify the questions Congress ought to be asking, many say.

"This . . . raises a series of questions for policymakers and those in the agricultural industry," says Catherine Wilson, an immigration specialist at Villanova University. "First, given the increasing trend of Mexicans moving into nonagricultural occupations, how can the US secure a steady and reliable flow of workers in the agricultural industry? And second, does comprehensive immigration reform legislation provide a time-sensitive and effective response to this phenomenon?"

The answers to those questions could push the US toward working with illegal immigrants already in the country, some say.

"The boom in Mexican immigration is over. Mexico's rural sector is declining, labor force growth is decelerating, Mexico is becoming an aging society, its middle class is expanding, and incomes are rising," says Douglas Massey, a sociologist at the Woodrow Wilson School of Public and International Affairs at Princeton University in New Jersey. "The critical need at this point is some kind of legalization for those already here."

Reducing Economic Migration

Others caution against making too much of the research right away, suggesting that the Mexican developments need to be seen in the larger context of events in the region.

"Things are changing in Mexico in ways that will fundamentally change the migration patterns that have been in place for over a century, but that doesn't mean things will end overnight," says Lisa García Bedolla, chairwoman of the Center for Latino Policy Research at the University of California, Berkeley.

After all, what is happening economically and politically in Mexico is somewhat the opposite of what's happening in other parts of Central America, she says. So while the numbers of

Mexican workers may decline, numbers of workers from other Central American countries might not.

According to Pew Research, 57 percent of illegal immigrants already in America are Mexican.

In the end, what the study does show is that border enforcement is much less effective in controlling illegal immigration than economic conditions abroad, says Bill Ong Hing, a professor at the University of San Francisco School of Law.

The bipartisan bill in the Senate allocates an additional $6.5 billion for border enforcement. "Those funds would be spent so much more wisely and effectively on helping Mexico with its economy," says Professor Hing. "The notion of a strong border may sound appealing, but a strong Mexican economy is the real way to reduce economic migration."

Organizations to Contact

The editors have compiled the following list of organizations concerned with the issues debated in this book. The descriptions are derived from materials provided by the organizations. All have publications or information available for interested readers. The list was compiled on the date of publication of the present volume; the information here may change. Be aware that many organizations take several weeks or longer to respond to inquiries, so allow as much time as possible.

American Immigration Council
1331 G St. NW, Suite 200, Washington, DC 20005-3141
(202) 507-7500 • fax: (202) 742-5619
website: www.americanimmigrationcouncil.org

The American Immigration Council, formerly called the American Immigration Law Foundation, was established in 1987 as an nonprofit educational and charitable organization. The Council seeks to strengthen America by honoring our immigrant history and promoting prosperity and cultural richness by educating citizens about immigrant contributions, advocating for humane immigration policies that comply with fundamental constitutional and human rights, and working for justice and fairness for immigrants. The group's website includes an Immigration Policy Center that features a list of immigration issues, press releases, and a blog. Publications include *A Guide to S. 744: Understanding the 2013 Senate Immigration Bill* and *Crafting a Successful Legalization Program: Lessons from the Past*. Examples of recent blogs include "Local Welcoming Initiatives Help Build a Nation of Neighbors" and "Immigrants Boost Economic Vitality through the Housing Market."

America's Voice (AV)
1050 17th St. NW, Suite 490, Washington, DC 20036
(202) 463-8602
website: http://americasvoiceonline.org

America's Voice (AV) is an organization that advocates for immigration policy changes that guarantee full labor, civil, and political rights for immigrants and their families. AV works in partnership with progressive, faith-based, labor, civil rights, grassroots groups, networks, and leaders to enact federal legislation to grant full citizenship to the nation's eleven million undocumented immigrants. The AV website features a blog, public polling information, research, political assessments, press releases, and news reports. Examples of the types of publications available here include "New Poll: Latino 'Presidential' Voters on Potential 2016 Candidates and the Role of Immigration Reform" and "Highlights and 'Lowlights' of the Bipartisan Senate Immigration Bill."

Center for American Progress (CAP)
1333 H St. NW, 10th Floor, Washington, DC 20005
(202) 682-1611
website: www.americanprogress.org

The Center for American Progress (CAP) is a progressive think tank founded in 2003 that focuses on a variety of issues, including energy, national security, economic growth and opportunity, education, health care, and immigration. CAP has been very active in the immigration debate and has advocated for a path to citizenship for undocumented immigrants. The group also supports the Senate immigration reform proposal. Under the immigration tab on the group's website, readers can find numerous fact sheets, articles, reports, and other publications on the immigration issue. Examples include "The Top 5 Things the Senate Immigration Reform Bill Accomplishes," "The 6 Key Takeaways from the CBO Cost Estimate of S. 744," and "Immigrants and Their Children in the Future American Workforce."

Center for Immigration Studies (CIS)
1629 K St. NW, Suite 600, Washington, DC 20006
(202) 466-8185 • fax: (202) 466-8076
website: www.cis.org

The Center for Immigration Studies (CIS) is an independent, nonpartisan, nonprofit, research organization founded in 1985 to provide immigration policy makers, the academic community, news media, and concerned citizens with information about the social, economic, environmental, security, and fiscal consequences of legal and illegal immigration into the United States. The Center's website is a rich source of blogs, magazine articles, and op-eds about many different immigration issues, including illegal immigration, legal immigration, the DREAM Act, the Senate immigration reform proposal, and others. The website also has a publications tab that sends the researcher to all Center publications, announcements, congressional testimony, and panel discussion transcripts dating back to 1986. Some examples of recent publications include *Amnesty Bill No Benefit to American Workers*; *Immigrant Gains and Native Losses in the Job Market, 2000 to 2013*; and *Liberal Voices on Immigration and U.S. Workers.*

Federation for American Immigration Reform (FAIR)
25 Massachusetts Ave. NW, Suite 330, Washington, DC 20001
(202) 328-7004 • fax: (202) 387-3447
website: www.fairus.org

The Federation for American Immigration Reform (FAIR) is a national nonprofit, public-interest, and membership organization that seeks to reform the nation's immigration policies by improving border security, stopping illegal immigration, and lowering immigration levels to about three hundred thousand a year. The group's website contains a wealth of information about various facets of the immigration issue, including illegal immigration, legal immigration, labor and economics, guest workers, immigration reform legislation, and population and societal concerns. Publications available on the website include numerous reports, an immigration reform newsletter called *Immigration Report*, press releases, opinion articles, blogs, and congressional testimony.

The Heritage Foundation
214 Massachusetts Ave. NE, Washington, DC 20002-4999
(202) 546-4400
website: www.heritage.org

The Heritage Foundation is a conservative think tank founded in 1973 to promote conservative public policies based on the principles of free enterprise, limited government, individual freedom, traditional American values, and a strong national defense. Immigration is one of the many key issues listed on the group's website, and the Foundation opposes amnesty for undocumented immigrants and has worked to defeat the immigration reform approach contained in the Senate immigration reform bill. A number of publications on immigration are available from this website, including, for example, reports such as *The Fiscal Cost of Amnesty to U.S. Taxpayers* and *Immigration Bill Doesn't Secure the Border.*

United We Dream (UWD)
1900 L St. NW, Suite 900, Washington, DC 20036
e-mail: info@unitedwedream.org
website: http://unitedwedream.org

United We Dream (UWD) is an immigrant youth-led organization made up of a network of fifty-two affiliate organizations in twenty-five states. The group organizes and advocates for the dignity and fair treatment of immigrant youth and families, regardless of immigration status. UWD seeks to win citizenship for the entire undocumented community and end deportations and abuses. The group's website provides information to immigrants seeking to apply for DACA and is a source of news and information about immigration reform legislation. Publications include updates about legislation and court decisions and news articles that reference UWD.

US Immigration and Customs Enforcement (ICE)
500 12th St. SW, Washington, DC 20536
(202) 732-4242
website: www.ice.gov/index.htm

The US Immigration and Customs Enforcement is the main investigative arm of the US Department of Homeland Security (DHS), a federal agency charged with enforcing US immigration laws. ICE was created in 2003 through a merger of the investigative and interior enforcement elements of the US Customs Service and the Immigration and Naturalization Service. DHS in recent years has reformed immigration enforcement, prioritizing the removal of criminal aliens who pose a threat to public safety and targeting employers who knowingly and repeatedly break the law. The ICE website and library contain useful information about agency activities and enforcement, as well as news releases, reports, speeches, and testimonies. Fact sheets, for example, are available on issues such as the agency's Criminal Alien Program, Detainee Health Care, and Detention Standards.

Bibliography

Books

Jeb Bush and Clint Bolick	*Immigration Wars: Forging an American Solution*. New York: Threshold Editions, 2013.
Julie Dowling and Jonathan Inda	*Governing Immigration Through Crime: A Reader*. Stanford, CA: Stanford Social Sciences, 2013.
Judith Gans, Elaine M. Replogle, and Daniel J. Tichenor, eds.	*Debates on U.S. Immigration*. Thousand Oaks, CA: SAGE Publications, 2012.
David A. Gerber	*American Immigration: A Very Short Introduction*. New York: Oxford University Press, 2011.
Tanya Maria Golash-Boza	*Immigration Nation: Raids, Detentions, and Deportations in Post-9/11 America*. Boulder, CO: Paradigm Publications, 2012.
Jose H. Gomez	*Immigration and the Next America: Renewing the Soul of Our Nation*. Huntingdon, IN: Our Sunday Visitor, 2013.
Richard N. Haass	*Foreign Policy Begins at Home: The Case for Putting America's House in Order*. New York: Basic Books, 2013.

Jennifer L. Hochschild, Vesla M. Weaver, and Traci R. Burch — *Creating a New Racial Order: How Immigration, Multiracialism, Genomics, and the Young Can Remake Race in America*. Princeton, NJ: Princeton University Press, 2012.

Kevin R. Johnson and Bernard Trujillo — *Immigration Law and the U.S.-Mexico Border: Si se puede?* Tucson: University of Arizona Press, 2011.

Marie Friedmann Marquardt et al. — *Living "Illegal": The Human Face of Unauthorized Immigration*. New York: New Press, 2011.

Pilar Marrero — *Killing the American Dream: How Anti-Immigration Extremists Are Destroying the Nation*. Basingstoke, UK: Palgrave Macmillan, 2012.

Lisa Patel — *Youth Held at the Border: Immigration, Education, and the Politics of Inclusion*. New York: Teachers College Press, 2012.

J.D. Payne and Jason Mandryk — *Strangers Next Door: Immigration, Migration and Mission*. Downers Grove, IL: IVP Books, 2012.

Peter Schrag — *Not Fit for Our Society: Immigration and Nativism in America*. Berkeley: University of California Press, 2011.

William A. Schwab and G. David Gearhart — *Right to DREAM: Immigration Reform and America's Future*. Fayetteville: University of Arkansas Press, 2013.

Daniel Wilsher — *Immigration Detention: Law, History, Politics.* New York: Cambridge University Press, 2011.

Hirokazu Yoshikawa — *Immigrants Raising Citizens: Undocumented Parents and Their Young Children.* New York: Russell Sage Foundation Publications, 2012.

Periodicals and Internet Sources

Gabriel Arana — "Five Reasons Boston Has Nothing to Do with Immigration Reform," *American Prospect*, April 24, 2013. http://prospect.org.

Harry Binswanger — "Amnesty for Illegal Immigrants Is Not Enough, They Deserve an Apology," *Forbes*, March 4, 2013. www.forbes.com.

Mathew Boyle — "ICE Agent Rep: Immigration Bill 'Written to Handcuff Law Enforcement,'" *Breitbart*, June 12, 2013. www.breitbart.com.

Lanhee Chen — "The Immigration Issue Republicans Must Address," *Real Clear Politics*, May 28, 2013. www.realclearpolitics.com.

Adam Davidson — "Do Illegal Immigrants Actually Hurt the U.S. Economy?" *New York Times*, February 12, 2013.

Kevin Drum	"'Illegal Immigrant' Is Now Out, but AP Doesn't Tell Us What's In," *Mother Jones*, April 2, 2013. www.motherjones.com.
Elise Foley	"Immigration Bill Would Expand Dream Act to Dreamers of All Ages," *Huffington Post*, April 17, 2013. www.huffingtonpost.com.
Alana Goodman	"Conservatives Concerned About Immigration: More than 60 Leaders Sign Letter Pushing Republicans in Senate to Kill Bill," May 21, 2013. *Washington Free Beacon*, May 21, 2013. http://freebeacon.com.
Raúl Hinojosa-Ojeda	"The Economic Benefits of Comprehensive Immigration Reform," *Cato Journal*, Vol. 32, No. 1, Winter 2012.
Simon Johnson	"How Immigration Reform Would Help the Economy," *New York Times*, June 20, 2013.
Adriana Kugler, Robert Lynch, and Patrick Oakford	"Improving Lives, Strengthening Finances: The Benefits of Immigration Reform to Social Security," Center for American Progress, June 14, 2013. www.americanprogress.org.
Michelle Malkin	"Obama's Definition of 'Smarter Enforcement': None," Michellemalkin.com, June 12, 2013. http://michellemalkin.com.

Javier Ortiz	"The Time for Immigration Reform Is Upon Us," *Real Clear Policy*, May 22, 2013. www.realclearpolicy.com.
Marco Rubio	"The Immigration Reform Opportunity," *Wall Street Journal*, May 2, 2013. http://online.wsj.com.
Chuck Schumer	"Illegal Immigration Will Be a Thing of the Past," *Real Clear Politics*, June 12, 2013. www.realclearpolitics.com.
Service Employees International Union	"Framework for Comprehensive Immigration Reform," SEIU.org, accessed November 3, 2013.
Daniel Strauss	"Obama: Congress Can Pass Immigration Bill by the End of Summer," *The Hill*, June 8, 2013. http://thehill.com/blogs.
Sabroma Tavernise	"For Medicare, Immigrants Offer Surplus, Study Finds," *New York Times*, May 29, 2013.
Teaching Tolerance	"10 Myths About Immigration," No. 39, Spring 2011. www.tolerance.org.
Mark Trumbull	"US Immigration Reform: Why 'E-Verify' Screenings, While Flawed, Will Pass," *Christian Science Monitor*, June 7, 2013. www.csmonitor.com.
Erica Werner	"House Committee Takes Up Tough Immigration Bill," *TIME*, June 18, 2013. http://swampland.time.com.

Rachelle Younglai and Thomas Ferraro "Gaps Widen Between House, Senate on Immigration," *Reuters*, June 18, 2013. www.reuters.com.

Jessica Zuckerman "House Stands Up for Important Immigration Enforcement Program," *The Foundry*, June 4, 2013. http://blog.heritage.org.

Index

A

B

C

D

E

F

G

H

N

O

P

Q

R

S

T

U

V

W

Y

Z